THE POWER
OF THE CARPENTER'S TOOL
Moving Towards The Light

BASIL ANDERSON

Xulon Elite

Copyright © 2014 by Basil Anderson

The Power Of The Carpenter's Tool
Moving Towards The Light
by Basil Anderson

Printed in the United States of America

ISBN 9781498409933

All rights reserved solely by the author. The author guarantees all contents are original and do not infringe upon the legal rights of any other person or work. No part of this book may be reproduced in any form without the permission of the author. The views expressed in this book are not necessarily those of the publisher.

Scripture quotations taken from the New International Version (NIV). Copyright © 1973, 1978, 1984, 2011 by Biblica, Inc.™. Used by permission. All rights reserved.

www.xulonpress.com

Contents

1) The power of carpenter's tool 13

2) Predestined to be conformed to the likeness of His Son 22

3) Awaken to the immortal life within you 30

4) Metamorphosis power and principles that bring about change 38

5) Falling victim to the spirit of offenses 47

6) The power and benefits of correction 55

7) Harvesting from the seed we sown 63

8) Faith that inspires one to action 72

9) Called to embrace the sound wisdom of God 81

10) The assignment of your words 90

11) The strength of your belief in God's words 98

12) The power and benefits of making inquiry 107

Appreciation

My deepest appreciation goes out to my wife Ermine Anderson, for her support, love, and encouragement. I'm forever grateful to the Lord for placing her into my life; she has stayed by my side through countless obstacles. I'm also grateful to my children Basil Junior, Alexandria, Amaziah, Alexander, Avalon, Avionne, and Lisa. Special thanks goes out to sister Florencia Chang-Ageda and her family for their labor and kindness. I will be eternally indebted for their encouragement in helping me to accomplish this project. To Minister Riley whom God has placed in my life and ministry to be a source of inspiration. Also special thanks goes out to the Finding The Lost Sheep Center family for their endless gratitude and faith.

Preface

Unequivocally we know for certain that God has predestined every believer's life to be transformed and conformed to the image of His Son Jesus Christ, possessing and manifesting the Glorious qualities of His character and power in the Earth. Now, in order for someone to be transform into His likeness, they must first go through a metamorphosis process both inwardly and outwardly, yes, theoretically and practically before they can literally experience this change. Therefore recognizing that the process of transformation is irrevocable and can only be achieved through the existing nature of the spirit of truth and his knowledge. The metamorphosis principle is a none-negotiable course of faith, believing and studying, obediently applying one's heart, mind and action in the life's transforming word of God.

Why I wrote this book.

My sole purpose for writing this book is primarily to help encourage and motivate God's people to live a genuinely transformed life. Therefore, I consider this moment to be a great privilege in honor to the Almighty God, for allowing me to pen these words of inspiration, blowing the trumpet and sending a clear call to the body of Christ. I am reminding them not to take for granted their spiritual education and revelation, knowing that the illumination which they have received from His word is cultivating and strengthening their faith preparing them to stand their ground and succeed against the schemes of the enemy in all aspects of life. Also, one should bear in mind that every great assignment or task will require a season of preparation. Surely, this book is designed to help encourage you, and get you ready for the next level of living.

1

There are various kinds of occupations, and every occupation in this world according to its kind, requires its own specific set of tools. For one to be successful, one must be equipped with the right knowledge of how to operate that tool effectively. Everyone require the proper kind of training for them to be effective and to yield the right result. One can have knowledge of how to use a tool, but if one does not follow the proper instructions, one can get hurt or hurt others in the process. Let's look at an electric saw. If an individual does not have the experience in using it, that individual could easily harm himself as well as others, or even damage the tool itself. My focus is on the Bible. Quite frankly, it is the most powerful tool given to mankind. Fortunately, no one can damage this tool, but one must read it, to gain understanding, and practice its requirements daily. In so doing, one will become successful at all which that individual does. Life's reality will be enhanced optimally, and then they can certify to the truth that the carpenter's manual is the best book for all craftsmanship.

Carpenters are highly skilled and powerful people in the world. They are the builders of our nation. This occupation holds a special interest in the hearts and souls of Christian believers, because the Bible clearly identifies our Lord Jesus Christ as a carpenter. Not only was He a physical carpenter, but He was a spiritual carpenter as well. Every day of His ministry, He built up the Kingdom of God using His special tool – God's Word, which today is our Bible. He clearly told us in John 18:36 that His kingdom was not of this world and when He was tempted of the devil in the wilderness, He used His tool very wisely, thereby defeating the devil. There were many, however, who could only identify Him with

The Power Of The Carpenter's Tool

His earthly trade as we will see Him in the book Matthew 13:53-58 (NIV) that says, *'When Jesus had finished these parables he moved on from there. Coming to his hometown, he began teaching the people in their synagogue and they were amazed. "Where did this man get this wisdom and these miraculous powers?" They asked, "Isn't this the carpenter's son? Isn't his mother's name Mary, and aren't his brothers James, Joseph, Simon and Judas? Aren't all his sisters with us? Where then did this man get all these things?" And they took offense at him. But Jesus said to them, "A prophet is not without honor except in his own town and in his own home." And he did not do many miracles there because of their lack of faith.'* Many failed to see Him as the son of God. They only saw Him as Mary's son the carpenter.

Today, many are looked down upon. You may be such a person that is not recognized for who you are, but that is no reason for you to give up, because Jesus never gave up. He simply went to where He was needed and wanted. Sometimes, you may have to relocate or change the audience you are trying to reach. One's race, culture or background should not dictate to others whether or not that individual will become a productive citizen in society, especially when one seriously turn their life over to the Master of Creation for direction, because God himself will transform their life, and train them to become an excellent craftsman, and a powerful person who will shine like the stars in the universe.

God's Word gives wisdom. This is evident in Luke 2:41-52NIV, where we see Jesus at the age of twelve, when His parents realized that he had been missing for three days, they found Him sitting in the synagogue among teachers asking them questions, and verse 47 tells us, *'Everyone who heard him was amazed at his understanding and answers.'* Clearly, we can see that at twelve years old, He had learned scholars and teachers marveling at His wisdom, which we know comes from God. We recognize wisdom as the greatest tool God has ever place into the hands of His servants, along with the deposit of The Holy Spirit, allowing us to become undisputed kings, prophets, prophetess and priests or whatever profession is allotted to us in this world. Furthermore, when one let God's living water of life sweep over one's soul, there is no stopping that individual as to the level one can rise. Imagine now, the thoughts of the carpenter's son invading your imagination, allowing his tool to ignite good works within your heart. As such you will be able to receive thoughts of miracles, healing, forgiveness, deliverance and blessings, which will flow through you the moment He releases the presence of His Spirit into your heart, mind and body. With you believing that the Father, and The Son are always at work even at this time, every fractured area of your life will be repaired.

Jesus constantly did work for His Father and their kingdom. John 5:16-17 NIV reminds us saying, *'So because Jesus was doing these things on the Sabbath, the Jewish leaders began to persecute him. In his defense Jesus said to them, "My Father is always at His work to this very day, and I too, am working."'* Consistency yields manifested work. The more one uses a tool, the better one becomes at their craft or trade. Confidently, the conformation is undeniable, especially, when one personally experiences the reality and the power of the Carpenter's Tool for themselves. That is when their life's experience will be authentically testifying to the truth that the craftsman who uses his tools consistently, knows how to use his tools proficiently in building and repairing objects. The question that one must now ask is this: **Do I desire to become a well-skilled craftsman in this world, and am I taking my craft seriously**?

For Christian followers and disciple of Christ Jesus, who consciously know that The Word is used for training and equipping for every good work, how consistently do you use it? Well, let's review and concentrate on God's Words pertaining to training and equipping. 2 Timothy 3:15-17 NIV, says *'And how from infancy you have known the Holy Scriptures, which are able to make you wise for salvation through faith in Christ Jesus. All scripture is God-breathed and is useful for teaching, rebuking, correcting and training in righteousness, so that the servant of God may be thoroughly equipped for every good work.'* Millions of people have envisioned themselves working in a professional occupation, whereby they can have some kind of job security, a salary, and good benefits. In order for those applying for jobs or even creating their own jobs, one must become skillful in order to maintain a career or job in today's society. There has to be a training, before one is allowed to confidently master the tasks given, but one cannot be just task driven, there has to be a balance. To become well balanced and productive craftsperson, one must:

First: Become well informed about their craft.
Second: One must understand the power of dexterity.

The Power Of The Carpenter's Tool

A skilled person uses both mental and physical dexterity. What is in one's hand is guided by what's in one's mind. When one becomes skillful at displaying light on their craftsmanship then the world can see the finished product. Such combination is absolutely essential for the best result in any craft. Every individual, therefore, must be trained both mentally and physically before they are considered qualified to earn themselves an appropriate salary. Furthermore, man's wealth and achievement is totally contingent on their ability to continue to increase in wisdom and the craft that they are skillfully practicing daily. One consistently improves and increases their self-worth as well as their net worth, by staying prepared knowing that wisdom and skillful practice will bring forth success. For example, Let us examine closely the power of the staff of God that was in Moses' hands, and how he skillfully used it to bring about deliverance and success to the children of Israel, and for himself. Exodus 17:8-16 NIV says that *'The Amalekites came and attacked the Israelites at Rephidim. Moses said to Joshua, "Choose some of our men and go out to fight the Amalekites. Tomorrow I will stand on top of the hill with the staff of God in my hands." So Joshua fought the Amalekites as Moses had ordered, and Moses, Aaron and Hur went to the top of the hill. As long as Moses held up his hands, the Israelites were winning, but whenever he lowered his hands, the Amalekites were winning. When Moses' hands grew tired, they took a stone and put it under him and he sat on it. Aaron and Hur held his hands up–one on one side, one on the other–so that his hands remained steady till sunset. So Joshua overcame the Amalekite army with the sword. Then the Lord said to Moses, "Write this on a scroll as something to be remembered and make sure that Joshua hears it, because I will completely blot out the memory of Amalek from under heaven." Moses built an altar and called it The Lord is my Banner. He said, "Because hands were lifted up to the throne of the Lord. The Lord will be at war against the Amalekites from generation to generation."'*

By today's standard of technology, a staff would definitely appear to be foolish and insignificant in the eyes of the world. No one today would consider it as a powerful tool in the hands of an individual that could be used to establish one's calling. Surely, we can hear the echoing sound throughout the land saying, that's plain stupid, crazy, senseless even ridiculous. Some would go as far as asking, how can a piece of stick help you

The Power Of The Carpenter's Tool

to win a war and defeat your enemies? Can anyone envision our current president giving the general a staff to take the United States of America's armed forces to war against another country? Well beloved, these are just a few of the logical opinions and destructive heresies one seem to gravitate to whenever one is facing difficulties in today's society. But I am here to announce to you through the divine revelation of the Holy Spirit telling you, never underestimate the things that God has placed into your hands to use. No matter how insignificant or foolish it may look or sound in the eyes of the world, remember that God promises to use the foolish things of this world to shame the wise.

According to the preceding scripture, we clearly identified that the staff that Moses carried in his hands was a symbolic representation of God's authority and power. Surely, as long as his hands were held up, the Israelites continued winning the fight, but whenever he lowered his hands the enemy would win, but notice what his armor bearers did. They placed a stone under Moses, where he could sit. This placed Moses in a position of rest. Then they both held his hands up, one on each side. They steadied his hands and Joshua got the victory by defeating their enemies. We too must follow the same principle of resting in Christ Jesus in order for us to become successful and win life's battles.

The Lord instructed Moses to write this event on a scroll as something to be remembered, because He had chosen Joshua to become the next generation leader, for the Lord wanted to make sure that Joshua heard it. He knew that when Joshua heard this, it would be an encouragement to him whenever he was at a low point. Now bear in mind that God foreknew who would lead His people into the promise land so God specifically commanded Moses to make sure that Joshua heard about it. Moses also built an altar and called it "The Lord My Banner", which means that all strength comes from the Lord.

In addition, we also discover that true success is just not an individual thing but rather a collective effort. Therefore, it is wise for us to grasp the reality of such truth that we all can benefit from each other's crafts. Furthermore, the world is waiting on you, and for this reason we find it absolutely necessary to encourage everyone to be truthful and faithful in their calling. Continue aiming at becoming one of the best in the field of your occupation consciously believing and knowing that when you become skillfully mature in your craft, then it will start making room for you, creating the opportunity of a lifetime. We learn this from the wisest king on Earth, who penned the following words in Proverbs 18:16 KJV that says, *'A man's gift maketh room for him and bringeth him before great men.'*

Whenever man's crafts are able to move them beyond their fleshly ability and connect them to the supernatural, then those individuals will come to realize the fact that this is God's gift at work in them. For this reason, one should keep on pursuing to reach the highest level of excellence that one can obtain in one's line of occupation. By maintaining a strong desire of reaching the apex of one's calling, will always require one's time, attention and daily practice. Surely these areas are extremely critical for their growth and development because they demand one's earnest commitment and devotion of energy all the time. Now, bear this in mind, that it should always be the craftsman ultimate goal and responsibility to ensure that their crafts be beneficial to others, thereby those people can testify about the quality of their craftsmanship. Certainly this is the place where the supernatural ability exceed the natural, and the anointing breaks the yoke. Understand therefore, one of the greatest satisfaction a craftsman can achieve in this world, is not just the payment they receive for skillful labor, but rather the benefits that others truly obtained from their craftsmanship, consciously knowing that the benefits and the recommendation that come from those people who validate one's works, will always outlive the temporary reward.

Furthermore, let us acknowledge the real truth, that it is the Holy Spirit who gives men their skill ability and knowledge in all kinds of crafts. Meditate seriously on these words from Exodus 31:1-6NIV that says, *'Then the Lord said to Moses, "See, I have chosen Bezalel son of Uri, the son of Hur of the tribe of Judah, and I have filled him with the Spirit of God, with skill, ability, and knowledge in all kinds of crafts to make artistic designs for work in gold, silver and bronze to cut and set stones, to work in wood, and to engage in all kinds of craftsmanship. Moreover, I have appointed Oholiab son of Ahisamak, of the tribe of Dan, to help him. Also I have given ability to all the skilled workers to make everything I have commanded you.'* Without a shadow of a doubt or any hesitation, wholeheartedly, I boldly declare to you that now is the appropriate time for every believer, to listen carefully to the note and sound of the trumpet making its global warning. That warning urges one to become skilled at whatever craft one is called to do. The important key, however, is to be aware as a Christian that you have a great Teacher, known as the Holy Spirit and He will also help you to become skilled at your craft.

I am encouraging and instructing God's people around the world to wake up and arise, for truly the time has come for everyone to become skilled for the Kingdom of God. No longer can we tolerate or justify the poor excuse of people being ineffective and unproductive in their knowledge of our Lord and Savior Jesus Christ, especially if they have been born again for a long time. Every believer should develop a burning desire to become qualified to carry out the assignment for God's Kingdom while being here on Earth. Without proper training, one should understand the reality that they are not ready to perform their kingdom assignment. Speaking about an experience that would make one more than suitable to work in a position on a particular job assignment, and that every individual should acknowledge the truth that their only proof of evidence to demonstrate their qualification, is their training. In addition, according to the previous scripture verses, where we learned that God gave Moses a skilled craftsman who was filled with His Spirit, in all kinds of crafts to carry out his kingdom assignment. It was necessary for Moses to have skilled a craftsman in order to have been successful for the Kingdom of God.

In addition, let us take this opportunity to ponder deeply within our hearts and minds seriously the real purpose why Christ Jesus gave gifts to men such as the fivefold ministry. Ephesians 4:8-14NIV says that, *'This is why it says: "When he ascended on high, he took many captives and gave gifts to his people." (What does "he ascended" mean except that he also descended to the lower earthly regions? He who descended is the very one who ascended higher than all the heavens, in order to fill the whole universe.) So Christ himself gave the apostles, the prophets, the evangelists, the pastors and teachers, to equip his people for works of service, so that the body of Christ may be built up until we all reach unity in the faith and in the knowledge of the Son of God and become mature, attaining to the whole measure of the fullness of Christ. Then we will no longer be infants, tossed back and forth by the waves, and blown here and there by every wind of teaching and by the cunning and craftiness of people in their deceitful scheming.'*

The qualification of a trained craftsman, cannot be proven only by one's confession, certificate, or summarize resume, but rather by their skillful performance on a particular job assignment. Ultimately, action speak louder than words. Therefore, now by showing aptitude for learning, you have reaffirmed your love and commitment to Almighty God. God's consolations are more than enough to strengthen any feeble hands. According to the previous quote from Ephesians, we understand the true reason for the gifts that have been given to the body of Christ, is for one purpose only, which is to prepare God's peoples for works of service for His kingdom. Christians, remember that you are called to perform greater works, but before one can do greater works for the kingdom of God, they must first acquire training, a training that has been approved by God Himself. There are two sides to real Christianity, and both sides are absolutely essential for success. One side of real Christianity is to have a true experiential knowledge of God, the other is the skilled crafts that the Holy Spirit teaches.

It must be understood that each individual, in order to be successful in their work for the Kingdom of God as well as for their personal benefit, a personal encounter with God is essential. Jesus Christ Himself certified to such a truth publicly, by stating that the Father taught Him how to carry out kingdom assignment. Let us now examine that statement whereby you can draw living water to quench the thirsting of your soul. John 5:19-21 NIV says, *'Jesus gave them this answer: "Very truly I tell you, the Son can do nothing by Himself, He can do only what He sees his Father doing, because whatever the Father does, the Son does also. For the Father loves the Son and shows Him all He does. Yes, and He will show him even greater works than these, so that you will be amazed. For just as the Father raises the dead and gives them life, even so the Son gives life to whom he is pleased to give it."'* Consider that moment in time when the Patriarch, and the Son, Jesus himself, as well as the apostles decided deeply within their hearts to humble themselves and become obedient to the disciplinary training of the Holy Spirit, and to those who were in authority over them. Therefore, everyone who desire to become skillful craftsman or craftswoman in the kingdom of God must adopt the same principle and go through a season of preparation, whereby, one can become competent by having enough knowledge, skill and ability to perform their kingdom assignment at a satisfactory standard until they become an expert in their calling. Consequently, we must come to realize that without divine disciplinary training we are considered to be illegitimate children, and not true sons, which the Bible is very specific about, as shown in Hebrews 12:5-13NIV which says, *'And you have completely forgotten this word of encouragement that addresses you as a father addresses his son? It says, "My son, so not make light of the Lord's discipline, and do not lose heart when he rebukes you, because the Lord disciplines the one he loves, and chastens everyone he accepts as his son." Endure hardship as discipline; God is treating you as his children. For what children are not disciplined by their father? If you are not disciplined–and everyone undergoes discipline–then you are not legitimate, not true sons and daughters at all. Moreover, we have all had human fathers who disciplined us and we respected them for it. How much more should we submit to the Father of spirits and live! Our fathers disciplined us for a little while as they thought best, but God disciplines us for our good, that we may share in His holiness. No discipline seems pleasant at the time, but painful. Later on, however, it produces a harvest of righteousness and peace for those who have been trained by it. Therefore, strengthen your feeble arms and weak knees. "Make level paths for your feet," so that the lame may not be disabled, but rather healed.'*

Heavenly Father, in the name of Jesus, I pray that your people may not run their race aimlessly anymore, nor fight like a man beating the air. But let them become skillful craftsmen and women, qualified to carry their kingdom assignment. I strongly suggest that you read 1 Corinthians 9:24-27 also.

2

**Predestined to be conformed to the likeness of His Son.
(Romans 8:29)NIV**

Only when a person come to truly understand their destination in life, will they become confident in the things they say or do, otherwise they will spend time on wasted journey convincing themselves that the place they are is the place they are destined to be, not knowing it's not, and sometimes they are even too embarrassed to admit that they are spiritually lost and in need of help. Finding oneself in such a predicament can be very frustrating. It can leave one feeling confused to the point whereby they want to give up. I encourage you, however, to hold on a little longer and do not throw in the towel thinking that you are being defeated. Believe me, hope is in your hands right now, and God is standing by ready to release divine revelation and comprehension that is going to transform your life forever when you practice obeying His commandments. In addition to what has already been said, whenever an individual does not know what they would like to become in life, nor have any understanding of what God has predestined for that that individual to become, then life can be very hopeless for such a person. To find one's self at this juncture spiritually, mentally and physically is extremely painful, because having no sense of direction of where to go and what to do, can cause life's circumstances to make one become very vulnerable, whereby they are willing to sanction just about anything in order to get out of their difficulties. But the truth is, what that individual has not discovered, nor realized, is that the absence of the living and practical light of God's words in their life, allows the presence of evil and the force of darkness to come against them, clouding their minds.

There is no need for despair, however, because God has designed a perfect strategy which He is willing to reveal presently. A decision He made long ago. Yes I am speaking about a plan well drawn out, mapped out, and figured out, just waiting for your conception and execution in order to gain power and success. Consider these words from God as penned in Jeremiah 29:11-14NIV which says,

"For I know the plans I have for you," declares the Lord, "plans to prosper you and not to harm you, plans to give you hope and a future. Then you will call upon me and come and pray to me and I will listen to you. You will seek me and find me when you seek me with all your heart. I will be found by you," declares the Lord, "and will bring you back from captivity. I will gather you from all nations and places where I have banished you," declares the Lord, "and will bring you back to the place from which I carried you into exile."

Well many times I have heard believers quote this portion of scripture with great enthusiasm and a diehard excitement only to relate it to material possessions, rather than spiritual things first. By doing this, they miss out on the fullness of what this particular passage entails, because, whenever a person commits his or herself fully, to seek God wholeheartedly, God will strengthen and mature their innermost being with secret wisdom, which is far more valuable than any weapons of war. Once one has been imbued with the wisdom of God, that individual will come to truly understand their destiny as they start to develop from the inside, and no longer will they rely on empty arguments, nor will their hopes be disappointed because they will be filled with God's words, which will guide them to success. As one recognizes and accepts the facts that God has an arranged plan in mind for His children, a plan to prosper each individual child in all aspect of that child's life, each child of God will be able to trust God implicitly. Your cooperation, however, is extremely important concerning this matter. It takes an agreement between you and God to bring about the manifestation of His plan into an existing reality. First, your accept God's love and plan for you, then you can establish a love and devotional habit of obedience as a basic foundation passionately desiring to experience the fulfillment thereof. In addition, start making preparation by repositioning yourself mentally and spiritually to come into agreement with God and His plan for your success. It's clearly not possible for an agreement to be made between two individuals who disagree, as seen in Amos 3:3 NLT that says, *'Can two people walk together without agreeing on the direction?'*

The covenant of agreement that you have now entered must definitely be considered seriously, which you are bound to perform by obligation knowing that your success is totally contingent upon your obedience, while faithfully depending on God's wisdom to provide both spiritual and material needs, that you should expect and experience as you move forward in the relationship. In making sure that your life is clearly demonstrating and showing enough evidence that you are skillfully harmonizing in opinion and action with God and the Lord Jesus Christ, by studying His words knowing that the terms of the promises of God will be revealed to you through the scriptures. Conceiving and conforming to the terms of the covenant of agreement with God is powerful enough to transform you into His likeness, respecting and accepting the responsibility of the Holy Spirit to actively guide and direct you each step of the way. Please note, however, that any violation of application should occur during the process of carrying out the agreement, will consequently create stumbling blocks, discouragement, and delay of fulfillment of the promises, but remember these words, *"And thou shalt be called the repairer of the breach, the restorer of the paths to dwell in."* (Isaiah 58:12 NIV)

There is hope if you have violated the contract. Your immediate repentance, your change of heart from doing wrong, is covered by the debt paid by Christ Jesus. Remember, you are predestined for greatness. As you become physically active in God's words, by literally exercising your faith to establish a strong personal relationship with Him gaining access to experience all the benefits that come along with the new covenant agreement such as forgiveness of sins, the guaranteed deposit of the Holy Spirit, and the powerful transformation into Christ's likeness. All these everlasting values are yours, but they are also inclusive of earthly benefits as well.

Therefore, build now your life on these foundational principals which are eternal, understanding that your life is not limited to just the physical universe. Prepare now your hearts and minds to embrace the things and direction God has predetermined for you to become, and do in this world, as you examine this portion of scripture. Reading with intense interest from Romans 8:28-31 NIV that says *'And we know that all things God works for the good of those who love Him, who have been called according to His purpose. For those God foreknew He also predestined to be conformed to the likeness of His Son, that He might be the firstborn among many brothers, and sisters. And those He predestined, he also called; those He called, He also justified; those He justified, He also glorified. What then shall we say in response to this? If God is for us, who can be against us?'* After reading such a powerful, profound and trustworthy statement from the living Word of God, audaciously, I declare through the majestic authorization, power and revelation invested in me, and now to you my friends, that no more mental prison bars, nor any state of confinement, principalities and power, nor any institutional force of darkness can deprive or bind you any longer from God's justice and liberty which He has predestined for you, once you fully agree to conform into the likeness of Jesus Christ. Furthermore, please understand that the combined power of faith accompanied by actions, will allow you to experience tremendous success on all levels of life: Spiritually, Socially, Physically, Emotionally, and Financially. Most importantly, each individual must immerse him/herself completely into the immortal words of God by studying to grow and develop in the knowledge and understanding of His likeness, whereby, one can now put aside one's old attitude, behavior, and concept of life, which has enslaved some of us for years. Adapting oneself into the new and suitable character and likeness of the Lord Jesus Christ, means totally transforming, and being made new in the attitude of your mind with ever increasing strength and power through the wisdom and revelation that you have conceived and is acting upon, knowing that God is rewarding you for keeping the covenant of love, which you have committed yourself to maintain in your relationship with God.

There is undeniable power infused into the believer when he/she truly understands what is meant to, *'put ye on the Lord Jesus Christ, and no longer depend upon the basic principle of this world.'* This means the enslavement and veiling of the minds of mankind with obscurity, whereby, darkness prevail over the souls of men, has been lifted, by Christ

Jesus. Praise be to God who sent His Only Begotten Son, Jesus Christ in the world to forgive us all of our sins by disarming all powers and authorities that was against us. He concealed the written code of human regulations and offered us the privilege to be made free by the rebirthing of the truth in our lives, whenever, anyone turns to Him.

Give careful thoughts to these words from 2 Corinthians 3:12-18NIV that says, *'Therefore, since we have such a hope, we are bold. We are not like Moses, who would put a veil over his face to prevent the Israelites from seeing the end of what was passing away. But their minds were made dull, for to this day the same veil remains when the old covenant is read. It has not been removed, because only in Christ is it taken away. Even to this day when Moses is read, a veil covers their hearts. But whenever anyone turns to the Lord, the veil is taken away. Now the Lord is the Spirit, and where the Spirit of the Lord is, there is freedom. And we all, who with unveiled faces all reflect the Lord's glory, are being transformed into his likeness with ever-increasing glory, which comes from the Lord, who is the Spirit.'*

Once again, we hear the trumpet sounding a clear call saying get up, get ready, for now is the time for battle. Stop sleeping! You have been chosen to function in God's sovereign decision, which He has predestined for you beforehand. Remember, Jesus has removed the veil of darkness from covering your minds, so bring back your thoughts in view of reality by walking and acting in the likeness of God's Son, Jesus Christ. Appreciate with humility the transformation of Christ's image from glory to glory, day by day with an open heart and mind accepting everything He has predestined for you to become, and to have in this world. In addition, all believers must approach this process, and journey with confidence and humble attitude, knowing that The Holy Spirit which have been deposited within you is now actively operating through you, converting you into righteous people. Also understand that this process of work is clearly known as transformation of character, concept, behavior and attitude that changes believers into the likeness of Jesus Christ. So it is necessary for you to bear in mind that your ultimate goal is for Christ to be formed and developed within oneself, through faith growing toward maturity. Furthermore, for this reason, whenever, a new convert is born again and accept Jesus as their personal Lord and Savior, God sends the Spirit of His Son into their hearts guaranteeing their future.

The Power Of The Carpenter's Tool

It is time to meditate on this passage of scripture reading from Galatians 4:1-7NIV that says, *'What I am saying is that as long as the heir is underage, he is no different from a slave, although he owns the whole estate. The heir is subject to guardians and trustees until the time set by his father. So, also, when we were underage, we were in slavery under elemental spiritual forces of the world. But when the set time had fully come, God sent His Son, born of a woman, born under law, to redeem those under law, that we might receive adoption to sonship. Because you are sons, God sent the Spirit of His Son into our hearts, the Spirit who calls out "Abba Father." So you are no longer a slave, but God's child; and since you are His child, God has made you also an heir.'*

Stop for a moment or two, and imagine seeing and developing a mental picture in your minds, what your life could be like. Now apply it in accordance to the likeness of Jesus Christ whom God has predetermined for you to become like. When you faithfully believe that you have received His Spirit in your innermost being, and totally convinced of the facts that what is living on the inside of a you, as a person, will surely manifest outwards. By submitting oneself completely to the guidance and the authority of the Holy Spirit inwardly, is absolutely necessary for a person's transformation, growth and development, to help one to consciously meet those spiritual requirements that is guaranteed to produce outward manifestation. When one literally plant oneself in the living and active words of God, then the Morning Star will automatically start to shine bright within one's heart and mind turning the invisible into the visible. Consequently, one will also come to realize that one no longer has the desire to follow the basic principles of this world. We have to realize that there is an urgency about the time to settle down and concentrate on our ultimate objective in this life, which is to come into an agreement with God's words, by focusing and achieving all that He has officially sanctioned for us to become, and to accomplish through the guaranteed deposit of the Holy Spirit, that is now at work in all believers. It is the Holy Spirit that transforms us inwardly into God's likeness.

It is unwise for us to lose insight of God's vision and purpose, knowing that He has revealed Himself to us through dreams and visions according to His powerful words, and we will discover our ultimate destiny as we continue to establish a greater intimate relationship with Him. The following portion of scripture will enlighten us as to the privilege we have in

Christ Jesus. Let us concentrate now on Ephesians 1:11-14NIV that says, *'In him we were also chosen, having been predestined according to the plan of him who works out everything in conformity with the purpose of his will, in order that we, who were the first to hope in Christ, might be for the praise of his glory. And you also were included in Christ when you heard the word of truth, the gospel of your salvation. When you believed, you were marked in him with a seal, the promised Holy Spirit, who is a deposit guaranteeing our inheritance until the redemption of those who are God's possession–to the praise of his glory.'*

Surely, you can see that as you continue to walk in the conformity of your thoughts and your deeds in accordance to God's will, you will discover and conceive the secret wisdom about the things God has predestined for your life. By skillfully acknowledging the necessary step of action you must take to bring about the fulfillment of His plans, knowing that the chains of injustice have been loosed from off your minds supernaturally, by the divine portion, which has been transmitted to you inwardly, equipping you with renewal of strength, courage, hope and an advantage to succeed. This awakens you to the inner light of God's likeness, which He has destined for your glory before the foundation of the world was exerted in Christ. I now appeal to you to continue to seek, grow, and develop in His likeness to the point where you find great satisfaction to live out the fullness of His joy within your hearts.

Furthermore, wholeheartedly, I ask of you to pay close attention and deeply concentrate on this particular portion of scripture reading from 1Corinthians 2:6-10NIV that says, *'We do, however, speak a message of wisdom among the mature, but not the wisdom of this age or of the rulers of this age, who are coming to nothing. No, we declare God's wisdom, a mystery that been <u>hidden</u> and that God <u>destined</u> for our glory before time began. None of the rulers of this age understood it, for if they had, they would not have crucified the Lord of glory. However, as it is written: "What no eye has seen, what no ear has heard, and what no human mind has conceived" – the things God has prepared for those who love him – these are the things God has revealed to us by His Spirit. The Spirit searches all things even the deep things of God.'* This explains to us that what once was a mystery to those who lived in the past before Christ's crucifixion, is now being revealed to God's children, by His Holy Spirit, who has been deposited inside of us. God loves us so much that

The Power Of The Carpenter's Tool

He wants to share His secrets with us, so that we can have a prosperous and more productive life here on Earth. When we seek God by reading and meditating on His Words, we must also personalize the scriptures for ourselves being fully persuaded in our hearts without a shadow of a doubt that God has a divine strategy in mind of how to rescue His children from harm or danger, which He is ready to release upon us through the correct knowledge and actions of His Son Jesus Christ. It is then that we receive the wonderful revelation of God's mysteries.

In regards to acquiring His set plans and skills, one must put into practice daily, God's Words, in order to gain back the power and the advantage over the enemy and one's circumstances, knowing that this will spiritually arm and equip one for combat due to the power invested in one's life by faith. Once one has been enriched in every way possible, the challenges then become how fully one will be, in immersing oneself in that which God has predestined for one to become, totally allowing one's destiny to consume one's mind, time and energy with great expectation to experience the reality of His promise. Confidently believing in God's unfailing love for one's life will allow one not to be shaken, since His covenant of peace can never be removed. This guarantees that one's inheritance is undeniable, as long as one continues to walk in obedience according to the knowledge bestowed upon one by God, which helps one to conform daily to His principles and patterns of example, which He has set forth in the Bible; and since we are heirs according to the promise exerted in Christ, we have obtained the right to all the benefits as sons and daughters. Now let us move rapidly into our inheritance, recognizing and proclaiming the fact that the genetic qualities of Christ Jesus such as His likeness, attitude, behavior, appearance and personality, which, is the moral foundation of His character and spirit, to which we are predestined, through the guaranteed deposit of the Comforter whom we have received when we were born again.

Finally, now, concentrate on these words from Psalm 17:15NIV that says, *'As for me, I will be vindicated and will see your face; when I awake, I will be satisfied with seeing your likeness.'* It is truly my sincere hope and desire to see God's children faithfully come into agreement with the words of God, and adapt yourselves to His likeness.

3

Awaken to the Immortal Life Within You.

"For the bread of God is he who come down from heaven and give life to the world." (John 6:33 NIV)

Truly it was a joyous awakening that I experience deep down in my soul on that Monday evening of July eighteen, two thousand and eleven, when suddenly, the Holy Spirit caused me to realize the awesome power of the eternal inheritance we can receive within ourselves, through the precious blood, death and resurrection of our Lord Jesus Christ. An eye-opening, conceivable supernatural exciting reality started to develop within my innermost being stirring up some strong emotional feeling of excitement and gratitude. It was an influence that caught my attention, pointing me to focus carefully on things which are immortal. There I began to discover how God had strategically predetermined a victorious destiny for us before the creation of the world. What kind of a God would do this? My only answer can be, a God who loves unconditionally.

Therefore, I boldly command you through the secret power and wisdom exerted in Christ, and now invested in me to officially declare that the hour has come for the multitude who sleep in the darkness of the Earth to wake up from their slumber and clothe themselves with the imperishable gift of everlasting life that cannot perish, spoil, fade away or be destroyed. Redeeming God's children from their empty ways of life, which was handed down to them from generation to generation, is why

Christ came to Earth and taught mankind before He gave His life as a sacrifice. Truly the fragrance of life is now ready to come upon you perfuming your heart, soul and body transforming you to a higher level of consciousness of God's immortal power that Christ came to invest in us through His shed blood. Understand, therefore, that all statements made must definitely be confirmed by the enduring written words of God as stated in His Word – The Bible. We now turn to 1 Timothy 1:17 KJV that say, *'Now unto the King eternal, immortal, invisible, the only wise God, be honor and glory for ever and ever. Amen.'* Beloved, fix your attention on this spiritual vision of the immortal life for it is a guarantee. As we continue to have a heightened awareness in the awesomeness of God and His kingdom, our inner man will be strengthened with God's mighty power of truth, through which we gain valuable and practical experiences that go far beyond head knowledge. It is this kind of knowledge that transforms and fills us with the richest measurement of God's eternal inheritance. When this settles down deep in our innermost being, God's Spirit makes our body His permanent home.

Can we appreciate an immortal life if we do not know what it means to have one? Immediately, let us take a moment to recognize some of the definitions for the word **immortal**. According to the dictionary Immortal means:

1) Not liable or subject to death
2) Everlasting or Eternal
3) Exempt from death
4) Enduring or Endless
5) Continual
6) Imperishable
7) Incorruptible
8) Unlimited

To become immortal, or to become exempt from death or to live continually is a welcoming concept, until one thinks about the reality of living forever. What kind of life is God offering us? Certainly, it is one that will be devoid of suffering, sickness, poverty, pain, shame, depression, oppression of anything negative that we can think of. Whenever one is born again, surely, one is not regenerated from a mortal origin, but instead, one is regenerated from the One who is immortal, who existed before time was created. This immortality is achieved through faith in the ever-living and enduring Word of God.

Can you imagine the incorruptible and immortal seed that has been deposited within every born-again believer? Let's seek clarity by meditating on this portion of scripture from 2 Corinthians 5:4-5NIV that says, *'For while we are in this tent, we groan and burden because we do not wish to be unclothed but to be clothed instead with our heavenly dwelling, so that what is mortal may be swallowed up by life. Now the one who has fashioned us for this very purpose is God, who has given us the Spirit of deposit, guaranteeing what is to come.'* This portion of scripture tells us that flesh and blood cannot become partakers of the eternal inheritance. There has to be a transformation or a metamorphosis of our mortal flesh. This is the reason why we are grateful to Christ Jesus our Lord and Savior, because it is He who has made it possible for us to partake of an immortal life, by abolishing death for you and me on that old rugged cross. By dying on the cross at Calvary, He paid the price for our sins and iniquity, and by raising from the dead, He activated our access into the kingdom of God granting us immunity from eternal death through the light of the gospel. Jesus gave Himself up on our behalf for the purchase of our freedom.

In the following portion of scripture, we are assured that God made provision for us before the corruption began, to have an immortal life free of demoralization. 2 Timothy 1: 8-10 KJV says, *'Be not thou therefore ashamed of the testimony of our Lord, nor of me his prisoner: but be thou partaker of the afflictions of the gospel according to the power of God; who hath saved us, and called us with an holy calling, not according to our works, but according to his own purpose and grace, which was given us in Christ Jesus before the world began, but is now made manifest by the appearing of our Savior Jesus Christ, who hath abolished death, and hath brought life and immortality to light through the gospel.'*

Certainly, the unfolding evidence of the eternal, immortal, and invisible God continue to convince us with persuading truths and spiritual reality. According to the passage of scripture that you have just read, we recognize that through the death and the resurrection of our Lord Jesus Christ the crucified risen Savior of the world, we therefore, now are able to identify and connect with the promise of the eternal life and immortality through the revelation of the Gospel. So bear in mind, that Jesus Christ is our perfect and primary role model who was sent by the Father to guide us on this spiritual journey faithfully when we accept His instruction of discipline, which is a pattern of behavior and a practical habit of obedience that will condition our minds for success, knowing that faith is to believe and to have confidence in doing whatsoever God says. As we continue pressing forward to obtain an ever increasingly clear knowledge with a practical experience of God's secret wisdom, which is purposely hidden in Christ, we realize that we were destined for our success before time began. Now, however, the truth is being released to those of us who are seeking Him wholeheartedly. It is through our commitment and determination with thanksgiving that cause our hearts to have revelation, strength and power that they are conceiving while going through the process of being transformed into His likeness. When we consciously accept the truth and reality that ever living blood and resurrection of Jesus Christ is still depositing eternal life, allowing each of us as individuals to become spiritually fit and proficient whereby we are able to overcome the evil force of darkness, and the power of Satan. Upon receiving the gift of the eternal Spirit of God, every born-again believer is truly equipped and empowered with strength in their innermost being to become spiritually mature, with the guarantee that they can live a life exempt from death.

You may be wondering right about now, how can someone live a life exempt from death? Well, let us carefully examine a very powerful passage of scripture that demonstrated God's power in protecting the children of Israel in Egypt by instructing them to place the blood of sacrificial animal upon the doorposts of their houses for a sign of exemption. Exodus 12:12-14NIV says, *"On that same night I will pass through Egypt and strike down every firstborn both man and animals and I will bring judgment on all the gods of Egypt. I Am the Lord. The blood will be a sign for you on the houses where you are, and when I see the blood, I will pass over you. No destructive plague will touch you when I strike Egypt. This is a day you are to commemorate; for the generations to come you shall celebrate it as a festival to the Lord–a lasting ordinance."*

Here we identify clearly a very important tradition that was set in action to be practiced and carried out through generations, however, it was a temporary glory which existed for a limited period of time because the blood of animals could not meet up to the full measurement to redeem the souls of men. The children of God had to wait for the coming Messiah Jesus Christ, who would fulfill the eternal promise of God to totally abolish death through the shedding of His precious blood, providing complete freedom for sinners, and the opportunity for the world to be free from eternal death, which we inherited through Adam. Surely, in acknowledging the awesome truth of the following statement which declares, **"Salvation is found in no one else for there is no other name under heaven given to men by which we must be saved."** (Acts 4:12NIV), we are set free.

Audaciously, I declare unto you precious saints, through the invested power of God the Immortal Eternal Spirit, which was deposited, and now is at work in me through faith in Christ Jesus, letting you know that God has totally disarmed the principalities and power of the evil forces of darkness, which was against us from the beginning of time causing the soul of men not to enjoy anything good. I give praise to God for His immoral Spirit, which He has exerted in Christ Jesus, who is still officially offering consolation and invitation to the nations to come and accept the plan of salvation which He has provided for us universally. In addition, please bear this in mind that the Holy Spirit is a deposit one must first receive to be guaranteed one's spiritual inheritance and transformation of this world.

There is an invitational call which prompts us into action. It is located in John 7:37-39NIV which says, *'On the last and greatest day of the feast, Jesus stood and said in a loud voice, "Let anyone who is thirsty, come to Me and drink. Whoever believes in Me as the scripture has said, rivers of living water will flow from them." By this he meant the Spirit, whom those who believed in Him were later to receive. Up to that time the Spirit had not been given since Jesus had not yet been glorified.'*

Now, can you imagine on the mysteries of God that transpires at that special moment when an individual opened up their hearts to respond to the call of the Lord when He says, *"Come and drink from the River of Life that flows from My throne, and of the Lamb."* Confidently, I do believe that this is the place where God pours out His Spirit of Grace in abundance to those who heed the call, sealing them with His precious commitment of love throughout eternity by rewarding them with the promised deposit of the Holy Spirit in their innermost being, as an empowerment, guaranteeing their success in this world and the one to come.

Recognizing such an undeniable fact is extremely important for God's people's growth and development knowing that they do not have to struggle internally anymore to obey God's commandment because they have being equipped with the gift of the eternal Spirit that have been entrusted to care for them. Surely enough, the Holy Spirit has been given to all believers as a deposit, or down payment, guaranteeing God's commitment of love to bring us safely throughout this troubled world and into our final place of redemption. But we must first accept the reality and the responsibility of the eternal Spirit of God who has taken up residence within our hearts and minds. Understanding that He is able to guard, guide and protect us from the evil spirit and the dark forces of hell that constantly challenges God's people night and day. Nevertheless, we have been given the authorization and power to expel demonic spirits through the Name of Jesus, and by doing so, we emancipate ourselves from the bondage of sin and death. Furthermore, start making arrangement to now plant yourself by the River of Living Water where you will develop a burning desire to get acquainted with the immortal, invisible Spirit of God within, as you study and habitually meditate on God's Words. They will produce large amount of fruit in its season, growing and increasing into a richer understanding with much clearer insight of the knowledge of the Father and of His Son Christ Jesus, spiritually discerning daily between the temporal things of this world which are swiftly fading away, compared to the things that are everlasting. You must skillfully build your hope and life decision on things eternal, which must be your ultimate goal. In addition to what has been said, let us comfort, console and encourage our hearts and minds with these words from Revelation 22:1-6 NIV that says,

'Then the Angel showed me the River of Water of Life, as clear as crystal flowing form the Throne of God of the Lamb down the middle of the great street of the city. On each side of the river stood the tree of life, bearing twelve crops of fruit, yielding its fruit every month. And the leaves of the tree are for the healing o the nations. No longer will there be any curse. The throne of God and of the Lamb will be in the city and his servants will serve him. They will see his face and his name will be on their foreheads. There will be no more night. They will not need the

light of a lamp or the light of the sun, for the Lord God will give them light. And they will reign for ever and ever. The angel said to me, "These words are trustworthy and true. The Lord, the God of the spirit of the prophets, sent his angels to show his servants the things that must soon take place."'

Drinking from the river of the immortal well of life must be one of our primary desire and interest to prevent us from suffering all kinds of abnormal depletion, spiritually and physically. Millions of believers, however, seem to take for granted or ignore the consequences of being spiritually dehydrated, which leads to serious illnesses in the heart, soul and body. Dehydration is one of the root cause of physical death in the world today. Therefore, whenever a person's life is lacking the quality and necessary substance to function properly, then we know that the end result will be critical. Well you can imagine the man/woman who is living without the immortal eternal Spirit, how void or empty he/she is internally. Just to think about someone not being filled with such a significance substance that he or she was created to perform and fulfill their life's purpose is a tragedy. This is why it has been said, *"A man who strays from the immortal path of life will come to rest in the company of the dead."* Beloved, let us acknowledge the facts that without Jesus Christ, no one has the fulfilled promise of the everlasting life. Moreover, I strongly suggest that you should spend some time meditating carefully and seriously about these words from Jesus Himself in John 17:1-5 NIV that says,

..."Father, the hour has come. Glorify Your Son, that Your Son may glorify You. For You granted Him authority over all people that He might give eternal life to all those You have given Him. Now this is eternal life: That they know You the only true God and Jesus Christ whom You have sent. I have brought You glory on earth by finishing the work You gave Me to do. And now, Father glorify Me in Your presence with the glory I had with You before the world began."

Through these living words of God may you be fully persuaded in your hearts by firmly grasping and holding these records of truth to be self-evident that eternal life can only be obtained through the power and authority of Jesus Christ the Redeemer of the souls of men. The God who called us to His own eternal glory which He has purpose willfully in Jesus Christ, is more than able to divinely impart His covenant of love into our hearts and souls of believers. Therefore, upon receiving the precious gift of our eternal inheritance of all blessing and favor from God which is a solid deposit of the Holy Ghost power guaranteeing our success in this present age and in the age to come. Immediately, one must continue to nourish oneself with words of faith and truth, in order to continue growing and transforming into the image and likeness of His son, understanding that the ultimate purpose is to become mature in His wisdom so that you can live life fully out of the guarantee deposit God has invested in you.

Let us now seriously ponder this portion of scripture in 2 Corinthians 1:18-22 NIV that says,

'But as surely as God is faithful, our message to you is not "Yes" and "No." For the Son of God, Jesus Christ, who was preached among you by us – by me and Silas and Timothy–was not "Yes" and "No," but in Him it has always been "Yes." For no matter how many promises God has made, they are "Yes" in Christ. And so through Him the "Amen" is spoken by us to the glory of God. Now it is God who makes both us and you stand firm in Christ. He anointed us, set his seal of ownership on us, and put His Spirit in our hearts as a deposit, guaranteeing what is to come.'

The Eternal God and Father of our Lord and Savior Jesus Christ, the true resurrection of the hearts and souls of mankind, whom you have chosen, has divinely imparted everlasting life into His believers in abundance. We thank you for allowing us to come back strong and active in the immortal power and true existence of our spiritual purpose, being totally revived through the process of our transforming thoughts belief, and most importantly the continuous practice of our faith in your immortal words of life. Furthermore, Romans 2:7 NIV says, *"To those who by persistence in doing good seek glory, honor and immortality, He will give eternal life."*

May the mercy of our Lord Jesus Christ bring you into eternal life. Just remember if you persistently seek Him, He will honor you with eternal life.

4

Metamorphosis Power and Principles That Bring About Change

Time after time people do desire to see changes taking place in the following areas of life: Government, community, finance, relationship, our personal lives, and religion is no different, but we must first come to realize that successful changes depend upon one's ability to discover the truth about life. Often times we see individuals try to change the outcome of their lives with some old information which have ailed them completely. Many have tried hard to think positively, but that can only get them so far. Some decided to just keep on praying and believing God to come and do the necessary work Himself, which He has already done, and now is waiting for their discovery of the metamorphosis principles that is written in the scriptures, while others just refuse to embrace changes, but nevertheless, it is an undeniable process everyone must go through in life and there is no way around it. We can pay the sacrificial price up front, or spend the rest of our days in regret. I am fully persuaded in my heart that it is only when an individual goes through a refining process, the furnace fire of affliction that they gain such a wisdom and understanding along with an advantage of experience, whereby, they are well informed and able to make skillful and effective decision that would affect changes all around. Then taking responsibility to think righteously, practicing godly principles that guarantee their success and transformation will begin.

As we diligently seek to bring about successful transformation to one's lives both internally and externally, we seek our direction directly from the living Word of God. My true desire for those reading this book, is that the scripture may be understood in the light where it is pointing your attention to, so that you can obtain maximum benefits and satisfaction from the metamorphosis principles we are going to carefully examine and put into practice immediately. Furthermore, let us review and concentrate on this passage of scripture from Matthew 18:1- 4 NIV that says,

'At that time the disciples came to Jesus and asked, "Who is the greatest in the kingdom of Heaven?" He called a little child to him, and placed the child among them. And He said: "Truly I tell you, unless you <u>change</u> and become like little children, you will never enter the kingdom of Heaven. Therefore, whoever takes the lowly position of this child is the greatest in the kingdom of Heaven."'

Now, based upon what you have just read, certainly you will agree that changes are absolutely necessary for everyone to go through before any of us can enter the Kingdom of Heaven. Transformation is our prerequisite that qualifies us to reach God's standard of knowledge, experience, and skills, whereby we become proficient and effectively perform at higher levels, producing results in the kingdom. This happens when we come to recognize the fact that revelation knowledge is powerful, when it is acted upon, and when acted upon, we are made anew. Our radical transformation can only be made possible in our lives through the Divine and active intervention of the Holy Spirit who is at work in us as believers, supernaturally changing us from within. It is for this reason, the Word of God reminds us saying,

'Therefore if any man be in Christ, he is a new creature: Old things are passed away; behold, all things are become new.' (2 Corinthians 5:17 KJV)

The verse you have just read, reveals that it's impossible for someone to truly claim that they are a new creature for a certain period of time, yet still they have the same old belief of thinking, attitude, speech and practice or behavior. If one is indeed in Christ Jesus, one has been renewed in the spirit, and as such one's life will and must eventually reflect change or transformation. We must understand, however, that we cannot transform our lives without reeducating ourselves to the knowledge of God's Truth. Our minds have to be renewed about the things of God. Once we have been reeducated to think on the Truth of God, our attitudes, behavior, speech, thinking and practices in life will change. For example if we spoke negatively about everything and everyone, when we realize how much God loves us and how differently He speaks, then we too start speaking more positively, to reflect the love of God.

Throughout the Old and New Testament, we hear the prophets as well as the apostles of Jesus Christ, continually echoing the gospel call for changes. They urged political leaders, religious leaders and people of God to abandon their sinful ways and turn back to God and be converted. There are two critical sides which are important for people to work on, in order to bring about their transformation. One is cosmetic or the outer appearance, and the other is the internal structural, character or nature. The external is known as cosmetic, and the internal is called structural. Both sides are absolutely necessary to change, however, we see some modern day Pharisees, teachers of the law, both political and religious leaders alike, teaching the multitude to change their lives cosmetically by only decorating and beautifying their outward appearances. Their concern was based mostly upon how they were perceived, that is as – Religious Scholars- meanwhile, their insides were like empty graves, full of dead men's bones. This is what Jesus told them. We read this in Matthew 23: 25-29 NIV which says,

"Woe to you teachers of the law and Pharisees, you hypocrites! You clean the outside of the cup and dish, but inside they are full of greed and self-indulgence. Blind Pharisee! First clean the inside of the cup and dish, and then the outside also will clean. Woe to you teachers of the law and Pharisees, you hypocrites! You are like whitewashed tombs, which look beautiful on the outside but on the inside are full of dead men's bones and everything unclean. In the same way, on the outside you appear to people as righteous but on the inside you are full of hypocrisy and wickedness. Woe to you, teachers of the law and Pharisees, you hypocrites! You build tombs for the prophets and decorate the graves of the righteous."

The Power Of The Carpenter's Tool

Sincerely, this portion of scripture speak to every individual across the board. No matter what culture, class, race or creed we may be, our responsibility is to take some time now and meditate on it by personalizing and internalizing it. If we know that Jesus was so grieved to know that mankind would think themselves so educated, yet they had no change within themselves. They claimed to know God, yet they were unkind to God's people. They thought they knew God, but if they did, they would have been more concerned with the wellbeing of others, than with how others perceived them to be. We must come to recognize the truth and the fact that God's wisdom is the principal application for our internal and external transformation, and by applying the principles of God's Words to our daily lives, we become transformed into the image and likeness of Christ Jesus. By putting these principles into practice, we are guaranteed to have deliverance, success, and changes in our lives circumstances.

Now can you imagine what could happen when government officials and religious leaders unite together, joining forces with each other to bring about true changes in the lives of the people agreeing upon God's liberalism, a deciding principle that support changes both in politics and religion. Consciously knowing that both parties exercising power and authority strongly influencing the people's actions and conduct in society. No government officials would be exempt from God's commandments, neither any religious leaders, nor the people living within our nation would be exempt from the governing authority of the law of the land. Consequently, both sides would adhere to God's principles of wisdom and justice, which is the measuring line of righteousness, knowing that He has the power to endow the heart with wisdom and the mind with understanding because when the words of man's knowledge lack insight, we know that it just boils down to empty talk. Therefore, it's time to return back to God's constitutional principles accepting the facts that God is a Spirit of Truth, Wisdom and Justice, and a source of strength to those who believe and actively practice His command.

Let us carefully analyze the steps of King Josiah how he went about bringing transformation to his people. We read about this in 2 Chronicles 34:1-8 NIV which says,

'Josiah was eight years old when he became king, and he reigned in Jerusalem thirty-one years. He did what was right in the eyes of the

Lord and followed the ways of his father David, not turning aside to the right or to the left. In the eighth year of his reign, while he was still young he began to seek the God of his father David. In his twelfth year he began to purge Judah and Jerusalem of high places, Asherah poles, and idols. Under his direction the altars of the Baals were torn down; he cut to pieces the incense altars that were above them, and smashed the Asherah poles, and the idols. These he broke to pieces and scattered over the graves of those who has sacrificed to them. He burned the bones of the priests on their altars, and so he purged Judah and Jerusalem. In the towns of Manasseh, Ephraim and Simeon as far as Naphtali, and in the ruins around them, he tore down the altars and the Asherah poles and crushed the idols to power and cut to pieces all the incense altars throughout Israel. Then he went back to Jerusalem. In the eighteenth years of Josiah's reign, to purify the land and the temple, he sent Shaphan son of Azaliah and Maaseiah the ruler of the city, with Joah son of Joahaz, the recorder, to repair the temple of the Lord his God.'

We learn that Josiah was very young when he gained the position and responsibility of a king, yet he was wise enough to seek the counsel of the Lord God Almighty, and under the advice and instruction of the Holy Spirit, he was able to bring about reformation to Judah and Jerusalem successfully. He changed the structure of the people's custom both politically and spiritually, which made undeniable improvement. It brought about a restored kingdom, which brought about a restored economy for the people. The same principle should be applicable in today's world of decision making. Bear in mind that the master secret of King Josiah success was to seek first the kingdom of God, a powerful principle that is greatly ignored. This, Jesus urged us to do in Matthew 6:33-34 NIV that says,

"But seek first his kingdom and his righteousness, and all these things will be given to you as well. Therefore, do not worry about tomorrow, for tomorrow will worry about itself. Each day has enough trouble of its own."

We have clearly identified the fact that one of the greatest hindrance that prevents people from being transformed is just certain practice of tradition. Failure to recognize those obstacles, barriers, and impediments are detrimental to the growth and development of every human being. For thousands of years people have practiced the same old broken and failed policy of tradition refusing to seek new revelation that will bring about transformation as the king did. It is therefore imperative to duplicate successful principles that guarantee new outcome both spiritually and politically. Often time people fail to confront their challenges because of fear, lack of faith, and unwillingness to seek God's wisdom, because of this, they die in their tradition. The accuracy and reliable powerful result we get when we practice metamorphosis principle, which is the authentic principles that is in the scripture. Faithfully we know for certain that God's principles are going to change the physical form, structure, appearance and substance of all that needs to be changed. All this is done especially by supernatural means and power. Even now, God is supernaturally transforming our lives on every level: spiritual, mental, emotional, physical and financial levels.

Let us now set our hearts and minds to study the principles from Ephesians 4:20-28 NIV that says, *'That, however, is not the way of life you learned when you heard about Christ and were taught in him in accordance with the truth that is in Jesus. You were taught, with regard to your former way of life, to put off your old self, which is being corrupted by its deceitful desires, to be made new in the attitude of your minds; and to put on the new self, created to be like God in true righteousness and holiness. Therefore each of you must put off falsehood and speak truthfully to your neighbor for we are all members of one body. "In your anger do not sin": Do not let the sun go down while you are still angry, and do not give the devil a foot hold. He who has been stealing must steal no longer but must work, doing something useful with his own hands, that he may have something to share with those in need.'*

When God's metamorphosis principles become well established within one's hearts and mind to the point of transforming one's life, then, that individual become like a champion rejoicing inward being prepared to run his course knowing that he is fully armed with God's sustainable principles, courage and strength for battle whereby, he can now centralize nations, government, and religious organizations. When one becomes proficient in the Word of God, one can accomplish, what would ordinarily seem impossible. In addition, this proficiency can only be achieved through daily devotion and by being disciplined. Everyone has the opportunity to be reinstated back into their original position God has for them. This can be achieved by learning to reestablish themselves in an intimate personal relationship with God, by adapting themselves with the metamorphosis principle that guarantees transformation across the board when it is fully exercised.

When a person discovers the true benefits of intelligence then they will continue to seek to become academically equipped, and fit to perform at a higher level in the kingdom of God. Constantly we are reminded that people are being destroyed for lack of knowledge and understanding, which is necessary to transform their lives. Let us carefully examine Paul's conversion and testimony which is documented in Galatians 1:11-18NIV:

'I want you to know, brothers and sisters, that the gospel preach is not of human origin. I did not receive it from any man, nor was I taught it; rather, I received it by revelation from Jesus Christ. For you have heard of my previous way of life in Judaism, how intensely I persecuted the church of God and tried to destroy it. I was advancing in Judaism beyond many Jews of my own age and was extremely zealous for the traditions of my fathers. But when God, who set me apart from my mother's womb and called me by His grace, was pleased to reveal His Son in me so that I might preach Him among the Gentiles, my immediate response was not to consult any human being. I did not go up to Jerusalem to see those who were apostles before I was, but I went into Arabia. Later returned to Damascus. Then after three years, I went up to Jerusalem to get acquainted with Cephas and stayed with him fifteen days.'

After carefully examining the Apostle Paul's conversion and testimony, it should automatically enlarge the capacity and size of one's vision, faith, expectation, courage and confidence in the revelation knowledge of God's metamorphosis principles that bring about transformation upon practice or the habit of obedience. In addition, when the promise gift of the Holy Spirit and the testimony of His words have been definitely confirmed within one's lives, then we know for certain that they have been endowed with power from above. Nevertheless, we must continue to yield ourselves to the desire for change, fully indulging in the practice of the metamorphosis principles that have been established in the scriptures in order to bring about transformation in our lives. There are three major categories we must strongly focus our attention on when we desire change:

1) In the area of seeking God's knowledge and wisdom.
2) In the area of our appearance/representation of Him
3) In the area of our practice/habits of work.

Daily invoking these metamorphosis principles with earnest expectation, consciously knowing that these prevailing principles are irrevocable, unalterable and sanctioned by God Himself. Therefore, blessed is the individual who can discern his error, then true transformation will take effect when they apply the metamorphosis principles to their circumstances.

Now get ready and start aiming for a mountain top experience of transfiguration to take place in your life. As you carefully examine what Jesus, clearly demonstrated to Peter, James and John in Luke 9:28-36 NIV which says,

'About eight days after Jesus said this, He took Peter, John and James with Him and went up onto a mountain to pray. As He was praying, the appearance of his face changed, and his clothes became as bright as a flash of lightning. Two men, Moses and Elijah appeared in glorious splendor, talking with Jesus. They spoke about his departure, which he was about to bring to fulfillment at Jerusalem. Peter and his companions were very sleepy, but when they became fully awake, they saw his glory and the two men standing with him. As the men were leaving Jesus, Peter said to Him, "Master, it is good for us to be here. Let us put up three shelters–one for you, one for Moses and one for Elijah." (He did not know what He was saying.) While he was speaking, a cloud appeared and covered them, and they were afraid as they entered the cloud. A voice came from the cloud saying, "This is My Son whom I have chosen; listen to Him." When the voice had spoken, they found

that Jesus was alone. The disciples kept this to themselves and did not tell anyone at that time what they had seen."

What we have learned from this portion of scripture is that we understand what Jesus had demonstrated in front of Peter, James and John, was documented as an event because He is fully God as well as He was fully man. However, our personal transformation is not an event, rather it is a progressive process. Also it is contingent upon one's practical obedience, by faithfully and carefully listening to God's instructions and daily applying the metamorphosis principles that would bring about solution. Everyone should develop an effective problem solving system which they then apply to any situation that they are facing. Firstly, one should carefully define their problem and then lay out the basic metamorphosis principle necessary to bring about the solution you desire. For example, there are many important steps individuals should follow:

1) You must write down a clear definition of the problem
2) Make a list of the biblical principles and truths that you are going to use to bring about the solution or change
3) Make sure the principles which you are going to apply will also change your attitude and actions in order to bring about a complete desired solution.

Please ponder these words over. Romans 12:1-2 NIV says,

'Therefore, I urge you, brothers and sisters, in view of God's mercy to offer your bodies as a living sacrifice, holy and pleasing to God–this is your true and proper worship. DO NOT conform to the pattern of this world, but be transformed by the renewing of your mind. Then you will be able to test and approve what God's will is–His good, pleasing and perfect will.'

5

Millions fall victim to the spirit of offences: James 1:20NIV states, "...Because human anger does not produce the righteousness that God desires."

Spiritually traveling through the road of creation in response to the Father's calling can be very challenging at times, especially when an individual does not have sufficient amount of experience and knowledge to sustain them on their journey. Being in such a position can be frightening. A feeling of discouragement, frustration, confusion, and ignorance can easily capture one's attention and put a wicked stumbling block in their way. Intellectual weakness is Satan's simple strategy for keeping individuals in bondage. Does the wiles of the enemy continue to prevail in the lives of believers as well as unbelievers? Certainly, millions are still uninformed and unaware of Satan's beguiling tricks, while others seems to love the practice of deceitfulness. After carefully analyzing the reason that suddenly interrupt people's destiny, one of the most outstanding causes that I constantly come upon, is the spirit of offenses. It destroys relationships across the board such as marriages, businesses, churches, families, and friendships. It is a disagreeable and aggressive attitude and action the ruler of darkness keeps on implementing. Unfortunately, millions of people do not recognize there is a deceiving trick that the enemy is using to gain advantage over us as believers engaging in this spiritual warfare of life. It is the enemy's motive is to keep us separated from each other, but most importantly from the unity of the faith and the love of God. Let us review some of the definition of the word '**offense**':

a. A sin that cause one to stumble
b. Crime
c. Transgress the moral divine law
d. Hurtful feeling
e. Resentment
f. Dislike/vexation
g. Displeasure/make angry
h. Attack/insult

All these definitions can be summed up as unacceptable. A delinquency of spiritual and social behavior. Oftentimes we cause someone to be angry, sometime it's through the good or bad things we do or say. Sometimes well meaning intentions can surely be perceived in the wrong way. For example, let us carefully examine Cain's reaction toward his younger Able. Genesis 4:2-9NIV states:

'Later she gave birth to his brother Able. Now Able kept flocks and Cain worked the soil. In the course of time Cain brought some of the fruits of the soil as an offering to the Lord. And Able also brought an offering–fat portions from some of the firstborn of his flock. The Lord looked with favor on Able and his offering, but on Cain and his offering he did not look with favor. So Cain was very angry, and his face was downcast. Then the Lord said to Cain, "Why are you angry? Why is your face downcast? If you do what is right, will you not be accepted? But if you do not do what is right, sin is crouching at your door; it desires to have you, <u>but you must</u> rule over it." Now Cain said to his brother Able, "Let's go out to the field." While they were in the field, Cain attacked his brother Able and killed him. Then the Lord said to Cain, "Where is your brother Able?" "I don't know," he replied. "Am I my brother's keeper?"'

Instantly, a picture perfect image should start to form within the mind of one's imagination. In regard to that which you have just read, powerful insight, and information describing the true facts and outcome when one is offended. The reality of what actually can happen to an individual who gets caught up and tangled in the beguiling spirit of offenses and anger. In studying the above portion of scripture we recognize the horrendous error of Cain's downfall. By refusing to heed the warning of God's advice, he totally declined himself from submitting to the counsel of the Almighty God, who had warned him in advance about the spirit of anger that was crouching at the door of his heart, desiring to sift him, which eventually captured and destroyed both him and his brother.

Today, millions are travelling on the same destructive pathway, being manipulated and controlled by the spirit of offense and anger. Nevertheless, no one should be motivated by the evil force of darkness and ignorance, whereby they end up hurting or killing someone, because God has truly given us the ability to overcome the wiles of the enemy. How then shall we identify, guard, and protect ourselves from the spirit of offences? And unto who shall offences come? Well, let's calmly meditate on the advance warning Jesus gave us about offences. We read in Matthew 18:6-7 KJV:

'But whoso shall offend one of these little ones which believe in me, it were better for him that a millstone were hanged about his neck, and that he were drowned in the depth of the sea. Woe unto the world because of offenses! For it must needs be that offences come; but woe to that man by who the offence cometh!"

Undoubtedly, it is a reality that every individual will go through seasons of offences come what may, even being pushed to the point of retaliation, whereby, one is forced and ready to render evil for evil, but you should be very careful in such situation, because no one can truly fathom the depths of a person's offenses and anger. Neither can one withstand the heavy burden thereof. Sometimes it seems quite customary for some people to see, hear, and even read about certain conduct and outcome of individual, unfortunately, who has been deceived, and now operating under the influence of the devil. Let us not, therefore, assume, take for granted, nor underestimate the cruel intention and works of the enemy anymore. Frankly, it's time to accelerate your faith and mind to grasp this powerful principle as a lasting imprint in your memories. How to truly respond in the correct way to the spirit of offenses, as you prepare the way in your heart by examining this valuable life transforming lesson, taught from Joseph's life, who held no grudges against his brothers for all wrongs that they did to him.

Genesis 50:15-21NIV says, *'When Joseph's brothers saw that their father was dead they said, "What if Joseph holds a grudge against us and pay us back for all the wrongs we di to him?" So they sent word to Joseph saying, "Your father left these instructions before he died: 'This is what you are to say to Joseph: I ask you to forgive your brothers the sins and wrongs they committed in treating you so badly.' Now please forgive the sins of the servants of the God of your father." When their message came to him, Joseph wept. His brothers came and threw themselves down before him. "We are your slaves", they said. But Joseph said to them, "Don't be afraid. Am I in the place of God? You intended to harm me, but God intended it for good to accomplish what is now being done, the saving of many lives. So then, don't be afraid. I will provide for you and your children," and he reassured them and spoke kindly to them.'*

I suggest also that you read chapter 45 of Genesis, so that you can get further understanding of the story. After given careful consideration of Joseph's life story examining his reactions toward his brothers who deliberately offended him because of jealously, having the opportunity to reward them for their ruthless behavior, but somehow, he chose to deny the moments of evil, and show them forgiveness for their wrong doing. A gracious response will always stimulate peace and harmony, love and righteousness in the presence of evil. Oftentimes, we easily choose to operate out of certain old traditional belief and mindset, which does not promote the wisdom of God, neither is it beneficial to anyone. We cannot afford to continue magnifying the written code of evil that works against us. For many years Joseph silently suffered from the heavy burden of offense, the painful result of his brothers' evil intention toward him. Joseph managed, however, to overcome his difficulties successfully, both spiritually and physically, because he trusted God. The vicious crime of evil intent, and the stumbling block of anger and revenge were demolished because of the love of God being fully active and operating within Joseph's heart, and that changed the situation between him and his brothers. Please understand this, there are some past situation that we may not be able to change, but we can truly allow some situation to change us consciously knowing that God can and God will use some situation to change his people, but it depends on how we choose to respond to it. Just imagine the awesome outcome we can truly enjoy each day of our lives through the accuracy of God's principle of love relevantly applied directly to any situation that challenges us.

Let us continue to review God's words and see what we can do, so that we can have peace of mind in a world filled with offenses. Psalm 119:162-165 KJV says that, *'I rejoice at thy word, as one that findeth great spoil. I hate and abhor lying: but thy law do I love. Seven times a day do I praise thee because of thy righteous judgments. Great peace have they which love thy law: and nothing shall offend them.'*

Surely these irrefutable principles that have been established for our benefits, cannot be proven wrong, neither can they return void at any given moment–they are guaranteed. God's decisions of wisdom are undeniable. They can be fully trusted, having the confidence to consistently apply them in all circumstances of life. This is the key for winning the battle over the spirit of offense. According to the above scripture we clearly identify some foundational principles provided for overcoming the spirit of offense. First we recognize that the psalmist loved the principles of God's law. Secondly, he hated and abhor lying. Thirdly, he consistently immerse himself to praise God seven times a day. Then he publicly announced the victory speech saying, *"Great peace have they which love they law (principles) and nothing shall offend them. Hallelujah!"* Now that you have discovered some of the master secrets of overcoming offenses, you must no longer practice recompensing anyone evil for evil, but rather keep on reinforcing God's principles of love in all circumstances providing all things which are honest and truthful in the sight of man. Remember that God's ultimate goal for our lives is that we should live in harmony with one another if it is possible. Consequently, we know that it is very difficult winning an offended brother over according to Proverbs 18:19 KJV which says, *"A brother offended is harder to be won than a strong city: and their contentions are like the bars of a castle."*

Each individual should acknowledge the facts that it is dangerous using an outdated weapon that will cause them to fail and even lose their lives in combat. Surely, one must not be quickly provoke in their spirit, calmness that can truly lay great errors to rest. It is therefore, an individual's responsibility to try and avoid all kinds of extreme behaviors knowing that there is a proper time and procedure to deal with every matter. The true advantage of knowledge that we correctly apply is the result of wisdom, and wisdom will preserve the life of its possessor. Quite frankly, it is extremely dangerous whenever one's feeling of emotion rules over their wisdom. Self-control is when an individual takes full responsibility over their own actions and feelings. This is why it is God's ultimate design to prepare his people for any possible situation and trials that could happen.

Give careful thoughts to these words from Proverbs 24:1-4AMP that says, *'BE NOT envious of evil men, nor desire to be with them; For their minds plot oppression and devise violence, and their lips talk of causing trouble and vexation. Through skillful and godly Wisdom is a house (a life, a home, a family) built, and by understanding it is established [on a sound and good foundation], and by knowledge shall its chambers [of every area] be filled with all precious and pleasant riches.'*

We are urged not be overcome by the emotion of envy, which causes destruction, but we are instead to use godly wisdom at all time. If we continue to go through life using the same destructive patterns of wrong emotions, then the wrong mental image will continue to live on the inside of us. We have to come together to dispel the revengeful beliefs and feelings that we have been prone to for centuries. This can only be achieved through the light of the gospel. Let us examine David's response to his oldest brother who was burned with anger toward him. Just because David came down to the battlefield where he (Eliab) failed to defeat the true enemy, Goliath, the giant. 1 Samuel 17:28-31NIV that says, *'When Eliab, David's oldest brother heard him speaking with the men, he burned with angry at him and asked, "Why have you come down here? And with whom did you leave those few sheep in the wilderness? I know how conceited you are how wicked your heart is; you came down only to watch the battle." "Now what have I done?" said David. "Can't I even speak?" He then turned away to someone else and brought up the same matter, and the men answered him as before. What David said was overheard and reported to Saul, and Saul sent for him.'*

Meditating carefully on how David response toward his oldest brother offense and anger, I would like to direct your attention to few foundational principles which are essential when confronted by spiritual warfare. These biblical principles are absolutely necessary for individuals who are battling warfare.

The Power Of The Carpenter's Tool

FOUDATIONAL PRINCIPLES

1) You must be aware of who the real enemy is.
2) You must realize that you can succeed where other think it's impossible.
3) You must be well informed about the everlasting reward and benefits that you and others can enjoy.
4) Learn to use proven weapon and godly approach to defeat the real enemy.
5) Discover that you don't have to fail where others have failed.
6) You must understand you are not going to the battlefield to become a spectator or a cheerleader.

Principle 6 requires further elaboration. Definitely it has been far too long for many Christian believers, who have allowed themselves for centuries, to reside in the position as spectators or cheerleaders on the battlefield of spiritual warfare. Someone who thinks that their responsibility is to go to such an event to watch what's going on there, or just to encourage the crowd, is in mortal danger. Now is the time for them to make a declaration of intention to get out of those old mindset and start to adorn themselves with new spiritual thoughts that equip them as more than conquerors. In addition, true conquerors are always seeking to subdue and triumph over their difficulties and temptations. Primarily, their goals are to acquire victory by overcoming their obstacles by ways of mental and moral power because they truly understand the facts that spiritual warfare is not against flesh and blood, but against principalities and power, and the rulers of darkness of this world.

Before challenging the fight against principalities and the rulers of darkness in this world, however, we should know how to first acknowledge the truth that our offenses are many in the sight of Almighty God, and that our sins are ever with us. They testify against us when we choose to render evil for evil. Remember when we disregard the commandments of God, we are left without protection. Therefore, we will suffer great humiliation at the hand of our enemy. Nevertheless, the solution to overcome the spirit of offenses can only come through God's wisdom, fully operating in the lives of his people. Respectfully, I appeal to you brethren, to let your mind ponder this portion of scripture: Proverb 19:11NIV says, *"A man's wisdom gives him patience: it is to his glory to overlook an offense."*

Based upon the above statement, it is quite reasonable to state this fact that a hotheaded man is truly reckless, and unskillful when he is operating in the spirit of offense. We recognize that a quick tempered person always displays their folly immediately and therefore, misfortune pursue them. Seeking and applying godly wisdom, however, in all our circumstances is the key for one to gain control over the spirit of offense and anger. Surely, it has been said that God is no respecter of person. He has respect for moral principles. Proverbs 16:7 NIV remind us, **'When a man's ways are pleasing to the Lord, He makes even his enemies live at peace with him.'**

Here you recognize that God promise gives you peace with your enemies if you focus on pleasing him, so here and now let it be your ultimate goal in this world to always thrive to please the Almighty God in all your thoughts, speech, and actions. Consciously, knowing that his wisdom and principles are greater than any weapon of war, his principles of wisdom cannot be defeated neither can it be contradicted nor resisted by any adversaries in the world. Frankly, it just cannot return void when one appropriately apply it in their situation. Finally brethren, bear this in mind that it is to one's own advantage when an individual can truly overlook or walk away from the spirit of offense. Ponder these words from Romans 12:19-21 NIV that says,

"Do not take revenge, my friends, but leave room for God's wrath, for it is written: "It is mine to avenge; I will repay," says the Lord. On the contrary: "If your enemy is hungry feed him; if he is thirsty, give him something to drink. In doing this, you will heap burning coals on his head." Do not be overcome by evil; but overcome evil with good.'

6

The Power and Benefits of Correction – All Mistakes are Correctable.

'But who can discern his errors? Forgive my hidden faults.'
(Psalm 19:12NIV)

Millions today have swayed from the truth and are living in denial. They have erred internally in their hearts from the faith, and most certainly the word of truth has vanished from their lips. Therefore, they are now living a lifestyle of false pretense each and every day. Here is something that they should recognize quickly, that whenever an individual fail to acknowledge and correct their error, or even learn from their mistake, the true reality of the matter is that they have failed to seize the moment of opportunity to change their circumstance, and practice becoming a person of good moral character, sooner than later. By acknowledging quickly the error of one's ways, less time will be spent dealing with the consequences of erroneous behavior, and more time can be spent living a better lifestyle.

Imagine, how often we have forfeited wonderful moments of truth, whereby we can produce great results of honesty, but we end up missing out on the benefit of making things right or even better. Instead, we continue choosing to embrace the deception which we have come to believe in, thinking that we are making some kind of wise decision. Furthermore, many have conditioned themselves into believing that lying is the easiest and the fastest way out of their wrong-doing, especially here in the

United States of America. Basically, what they are doing is accepting the bait of beguilement as an attraction, thinking that this is the way of life, and that it would get them ahead faster in achieving their success. The real truth is, it's only taking them backward in life, instead of moving them forward. Some of them come to find out such truth the hard way when it is too late. Meanwhile, others never seem to learn and they continue to repeat the same deceitful pattern of behavior. We have to acquaint ourselves with one of the most powerful and reliable principle that each individual can sincerely depend upon whenever they come face to face with their error. It is the "Atoning Principle". This principle will bring about satisfaction and reconciliation. Everyone should always see, and aim to make an amendment for all their wrong doing, firstly to the Almighty God and secondly to the person that they are at odds with, by demonstrating godly sorrow through their action for the wrong which they have done. Thriving to restore harmony on all levels is beneficial to such an individual because they have cleansed their consciences from acts that lead to death and separation from God and mankind. Let us now concentrate on this indisputable fact about correction from Proverbs 12:1-2 NIV that says,

*'**Whoever loves discipline loves knowledge, but he who hates correction is stupid. Good people obtain favor from the Lord, but the Lord condemns those who devise wicked schemes.'***

Now according to this portion of scripture, automatically one can truly sense that the floodgate of Heaven is opened spiritually to us, gloriously pouring out an overwhelming quantity of revelation and inspiration which springs up from deep within one's innermost being. We see that it is a wise person who doesn't take offense to being corrected, and that such a person is favored by God. This should bring about thoughts of encouragement that is guaranteed to sustain and improve the quality of one's spiritual, intellectual, social and physical living condition. With the Holy Spirit supernaturally influencing believers to start applying God's teachings to themselves, reminding God's people to reform their ways and actions because they are only a correction away from the bountiful harvest of healing, deliverance and prosperity, which they have desired. Suddenly, then they would realize that this blessing was appointed from eternity, from the beginning, before the world began. Notice what the word of God said, ***"Whoever loves discipline loves knowledge, but he who hates correction is stupid."*** Well, just imagine when someone refuses to be corrected and what would be the outcome of their lives? Definitely, the reality and the consequences are unthinkable. For example, the determination of Pharaoh's unyielding heart, how he refused to let the Israelites go out of his country and because of the stubbornness of his mindset, the entire country of Egypt suffered serious consequences of different kinds of plagues in spite of Pharaoh's acceptance of being in the wrong. It did not produce the result of correction because correction requires works. Exodus 9:27-30 NIV says,

'Then Pharaoh summoned Moses and Aaron. "This time I have sinned," he said to them. "The Lord is in the right, and I and my people are in the wrong. Pray to the Lord, for we have had enough thunder and hail. I will let you go; you don't have to stay any longer." Moses replied, "When I have gone out of the city, I will spread out my hands in prayer to the Lord. The thunder will stop and there will be no more hail so you may know that the earth is the Lord's. But I know that you and your officials still do not fear the Lord God."'

Now during the time of the events of the ten deadly plagues which take place in Egypt, King Pharaoh and his officials refuses to honor God's instruction. Nevertheless, it has been made clear to our understanding that on couple of occasion Pharaoh did acknowledge and confess publicly that he and his people have sinned against God's command. The relevancy of this valuable lesson which we all can relate to in our own life today, is that it takes more than just acknowledgment and confession of one's sin to bring about real correction to our situation. Whenever an individual comes to acknowledge and confess their wrongdoing, the very next step that is required of them is to accept seriously godly instruction which is given, and immediately put it into action, then true correction will occur in their lives. Learning to forsake one's old destructive pattern of behavior is not as easy as one would imagine, especially, when arrogance and a sense of false pride has captured the heart of these individuals. It is manifested in them as a feeling of superiority in a presumptuous manner. Definitely, it is a false attraction that many find satisfaction in, and take great pleasure in such mannerisms. However, the truth of the matter is these stubborn and hardheaded people are always fighting against the Holy Spirit, but what these rebellious people need to realize is that no one can stop the redeeming work of a sovereign God. Therefore, when both spiritual and political leaders who deliberately decide to disobey the authority of God's command, they should acknowledge the fact that they are leading innocent people astray to be punished and are willfully forcing them to bear the painful burden by carrying the result of the consequences of the poor choices of others. This is exactly what King Pharaoh and his officials had done to their people in Egypt according to the previous quote from Exodus 9:27-30 NIV. Moreover, we can clearly see that misfortune pursues both leaders, and followers alike. When anyone chooses to despise the Lord's Word and break his command, surely they will pay for it whether the violations are made intentionally or unintentionally. Therefore, when leaders who are in authority made a bad decision the people of that country or community will suffer the consequence because they are automatically involved in that wrong decision-making although unintentional. For such a reason, we the people of any country or community have a responsibility to pray for the guidance of our leaders, so that they may conduct the affairs of our country or community with justice and righteousness. In addition, let us concentrate carefully on these words from Proverbs 10:17 NIV that says, '***He who heeds discipline shows the way to life, but whoever ignores correction leads others astray.***'

Now, should a man continue in his own folly and keep on ignoring the Lord's advice? Will he not accept correction from God for his life? Everyone must take heed to the serious warning against rejecting God's command. Yes, we can do so by seizing this opportunity right now, and start by doing some personal soul searching where you will spiritually examining your own pattern of thoughts, words and actions to see whether they are in agreement with God's Word or simply reeling against his teaching. Consciously we know that it is dangerous for a person to rely on their own insight or understanding for when false pride inflate the hearts and minds of an individual it produce a spirit of arrogance deep within them arousing them to overestimate themselves and underestimate others. This overwhelming pride is fully based on arrogance and conceit to the point where one shows too much pride in their ability and appearance. Therefore, their hearts are filled with the deceitfulness and vain is their imagination having no spiritual discernment whatsoever, because they have neglected the counsel of God and strayed from his commands. They are deluded into always thinking and believing in things which are not true. Their blindness continue to prevent them from seeing and realizing the truth that they have eaten the fruit of deception. Nevertheless, the good news for them remain the same forever. The ransom is paid in full for their recovery. Furthermore, I boldly declare that they shall be delivered from the snare of the fowlers and with joy they will draw living water from the wells of salvation as they ponder these words from Psalm 119:9-11 KJV that says, *'Wherewithal shall a young man cleanse his way? By taking heed thereto according to thy word. With my whole heart have I sought thee: O let me not wander from thy commandments. Thy word have I hid in mine heart that I might not sin against thee.'*

Realistically, the desired goal of the enemy is to see that a man's life is totally trapped in a mode of incorrect thoughts and speech that would exalt itself against the knowledge of God. Satan understands the outcome of incorrect thoughts and speech, how it produces negative results and behavior. Millions, however, have not yet come to realize such fact, that a man's life is trapped by their deceptive knowledge and sinful talk. It is for this reason that one thinking positively on the wrong information is deadly. Therefore, it is extremely important to understand that a person cannot correct their life by just thinking positively. To make true correction, one must first figure out where they have become twisted, trapped or stuck. Next, one has to accept that they did wrong and start seeking for the truth. Then, one has to appropriately apply the truth within one's heart and mind replacing that old conceived lie. In order not to be led astray by lies and deceit of the heart one has to skillfully practice replacing that which is deceitful in their lives with what's righteous and just. This is the way one escapes the corruption of the world. Often times people have tried their best to make corrections in their lives with the same old twisted and vain imagination from deceitful knowledge that have darkened their hearts making them become futile in their thinking. According to the above portion of scripture, however, it clearly demonstrates a vivid picture mentally to everyone, reminding us that we have not fallen beyond recovery, as long as we can earnestly accept the truth that

God has provided purification for every transgressor who has rebelled against His teaching. Surely, the enemy has poisoned the mind and intellect of millions, forcing them to become busy with evil thoughts. Satan willfully knowing that the effect of deception produces deterioration in the soul and conscience of mankind, but thanks be to God, the Father of creation for His unfailing love, who has made it possible for everyone to receive and enjoy the benefits of correction in their lives through the application of His powerful words in all aspect of our lives.

Now let us examine this powerful passage of scripture reading to find out exactly what is our responsibility and duty that we must put into practice immediately on a daily basis to guarantee a lasting correction and benefits for a lifetime. 2 Corinthians 10:3-6 NIV says,

'For though we live in the world, we do not wage war as the world does. The weapons we fight with are not the weapons of the world. On the contrary, they have a divine power to demolish strongholds. We demolish arguments and every pretension that sets itself up against the knowledge of God, and we take captive every thought to make it obedient to Christ. And we will be ready to punish every act of disobedience, once your obedience is complete.'

Immediately, we must take action and begin to refute all proud and lofty (carnal) idea, statement, theories, reasoning, and vain imagination that is fully based upon human wisdom and has become our customary practice for centuries. Magnifying such thoughts that exalts itself against the knowledge of God is wrong because it inflates the very core of our intellect, thoughts, that contaminate our conscience and spoil our true reasoning ability. Consider, therefore, how foolish it would be on our behalf if we do not exercise our God given responsibility to demolish every plan, method and scheme that leaves us empty of God's blessing. The false concepts that we have conceived and believed in, thinking that they are going to help us to win our battles, will not, so we must demolish them. God's mighty weapons, are still available for correcting and liberating our lives from conventional errors, opinions and beliefs. Furthermore, we have been empowered by the Holy Spirit to move away from the most usual ways in which the world think and conduct their affairs. Therefore, it is our priority and responsibility now to swiftly move into action and reform our ways and thoughts by breaking down every carnal plan, scheme and method which we have being deceitfully practicing throughout ages. Primarily our true aim and goal now is to transform our minds from being carnally-minded which leads to death, and become spiritually minded that would take us into life and peace through faith in Christ. Now having the ability to return to God's original standard of thinking, and building the mindset he intended for us to live and operate from the beginning of time. This can only be achieved, however, through the application and principle of His powerful words. Everyone must decide for themselves that they are ready to go through the process of demolishment; by being willing to remove the barriers within, and break into pieces every inclination of thoughts in one's heart which have been mentally holding them captive and forcing them to consistently rebel against God's liberating and healing words of truth. Definitely the enemy is working overtime to promote all his wicked scheme and craftiness, trying his best to prevent God's promises from fulfilling in people's live, and he does it by blinding their minds with lies and unbelief, causing them to think incorrectly and therefore they will not be able to see nor admit to their error.

Obviously, then God is our only source of power and strength whom we can rely on to escape the darkness of deception, and we receive His help by keeping in touch with Him, by meditating on His Word and by communicating with Him. Indeed, we must recognize the facts that His teaching and ways of correction are absolutely necessary for our turnaround. Therefore, it must be acceptable across the board in our government, in our religion, and individual lives. People who are willing to acknowledge their own error and rebellion against God's command – this mean serious-minded people who are ready to make the necessary correction that would bring about healing in their lives, others and their country, but most importantly bring glory and honor to the heart of God. Now without any delay, we must join forces together by agreeing upon the word of God, and as one nation under the leadership authority of the Holy Spirit, be willing and able to go forth and fight a good fight of faith, completely demolishing every internal and external deception that we have conceived through vain human wisdom and practice. Nevertheless, with a contrite spirit, we courageously come face to face with every concealed deception of sins that is hidden in our hearts and minds, we renounce and lay them down before the throne of Grace and Mercy as we confess them to Almighty God, knowing that He is faithful and just to forgive and purge us from every corrupt practices.

Let us meditate on this portion of scripture from Ephesians 4:21-25 NIV that says, *'When you heard about Christ and were taught in him in accordance with the truth that is in Jesus. You were taught, with regard to your former way of life to put off your old self, which is being corrupted by its deceitful desires; to be made new in the attitude of your minds; and to put on the new self, created to be like God in true righteousness and holiness. Therefore each of you must put off falsehood and speak truthfully to your neighbor, for we are all members of one body.'*

Undoubtedly, the power is up to us now, and they that love and cherish correction. We truly find out the way of life, we shall prosper and receive favor from the Lord but those who remain in their arrogance and pride are unwise, they shall suffer shame and disgrace for their folly. Let us take courage and continue the process with no intention of turning back, but fully determine to come in conformity with God's moral principle and standard of living, knowing that His counsel is in our best interest. It is quite obvious that we ought to leave behind the old corrupt life of sin and its deceitful practice, and put on the new self, by accepting real correction from the living words of God, which only guarantees benefits. We should understand the fact that correction is a slow inward process for outward manifestation in an individual's life. The truth is that we don't automatically have all good thoughts, attitudes and actions in the beginning stage of our new nature, but if we continue seeking God's guidance, and accept His correction when He rebuke us, having the willingness to acknowledge our wrong by making the necessary adjustment whenever He convicts us through His Holy words. It is then that we gain the formula of wisdom and understanding from His principles. His command is a lamp, His teaching is a light to our soul and the corrections of His discipline is a way of life. Remember these words from Proverbs 13:18 that says, *'He who ignores discipline comes to poverty and shame, but whoever heeds correction is honored.'*

"Father in the name of Jesus let us accept the fact that all mistakes are correctable and forgivable in Jesus' name. Amen."

7

Harvesting from the Seed We Sow.

Oftentimes people fail to acknowledge the facts that we do reap from the seeds which we have sown day-in and day-out. Immediately you may be thinking within yourself that I am a good person, which could be true, however, I have seen some beautiful people practicing some poor choices of principles throughout their lives, producing undesirable fruit from darkness, then they turn around and wonder why they are suffering and just can't seem to do anything right. Make no mistake about this, the word of God is precise on this issue. For example Galatians 6:7-10 NIV says,

'Do not be deceived: God cannot be mocked. A man reaps what he sows. Whosoever sows to please their flesh, from the flesh will reap destruction; whoever sows to please the Spirit, for the Spirit will reap eternal life. Let us not become weary in doing good, for at the proper time we will reap a harvest if we do not give up. Therefore, as we have opportunity, let us do good to all people, especially to those who belong to the family of believers.'

Most definitely it is clear to our understanding that we receive our harvest from the seed which we are sowing. Therefore, it is critical for us to verify with the three major kind of seeds revealed in the Bible.

1) The seed is Vegetation.
2) The seed of the Offspring of our body.
3) The seed of the Word.

Intensely now, let us review these three major categories of seed bearing plants on their own merit. To see how they produce enduring cause and effect in our lives, let us look at Genesis 1:11-12 NIV which says,

'Then God said, "Let the land produce vegetation: seed-bearing plants and trees on the land that bear fruit with seed in it, according to their various kind." And it was so. The land produced vegetation: Plants bearing seed according to their kinds and trees bearing fruit with seed in it according to their kinds. And God saw that it was good.'

Since the beginning of time up until present day, the land has produced and still is producing all our source of food, which is an everlasting blessing from Almighty God.

Now concerning the offspring, the second seed mentioned in this chapter, in Genesis 3:15-16 NIV, God Himself prophesied about the progeny of the woman's descendant who is going to crush the head of the serpent. Hallelujah! And now the divine declaration from God's mouth:

"And I will put enmity between you and the woman, and between your offspring and hers; he will crush your head, and you will strike his heel." To the woman he said, "I will make your pains in childbearing very severe; with painful labor you will give birth to children. Your desire will be for your husband, and he will rule over you."

And now I boldly declare unto you that you receive and exercise power and authority and crush the head of the serpent today.

The third kind of seed mentioned in this chapter is found in Mark 4:13-14 NIV, where Jesus gave the meaning of the parable of the sower saying,

'Then Jesus said to them, "Don't you understand this parable? How then will you understand any parable? The farmer sows the WORD."

Wholeheartedly with every breath of life within, let's ask ourselves this question, how powerful and precious is the Word of God to us?

Now that you have been given a glimpse of the three major category of seeds and their purpose, which is fully established in the Word of God, there will be further elaboration as you read. Frankly, stubborn refusal to believe in the seed of the living word of God will be very costly, because one of the major problem that we discovered in the body of Christ today. It is that most believers' dominant thoughts are outside of the Word, not acknowledging the reality that God is only seeking to perform His words in and through our lives. Remember these words from Psalm 107:19-20 NIV that says,

'Then they cried to the Lord in their trouble, and He saved them from their distress. He sent out His Word and healed them; He rescued them from the grave.'

The question now is, are you finding and receiving your healing and deliverance in the living and active word of God? Please decree and declare this statement of blessing over your life right now.

"I am a believer and receiver of the revealed seed of God in Christ Jesus. This imperishable seed of life is deeply planted by faith in my heart. Therefore, I am a harvest producing fruit bearing seed in the name of the Lord Jesus Christ in the land of the living."

I have asked you to repeat the previous statement because I am reminded of these words from Psalm 37: 25-26 KJV which says, **"I have been young and now am old, yet have I not seen the righteous forsaken, now his seed begging bread. He is ever merciful, and lendeth; and his seed is blessed."** King David lived by the Word of God and his testimony reveals the benefits of the Word of God.

Beloved, now that the light of the revealed seed is shining brightly within your heart, you must vow to continue to spend the rest of your days under the Lord's care, knowing that even when famine enter the land you and your offspring will still enjoy an abundance of fruit. However, for anyone to produce godly success, they cannot allow or afford their thoughts to stray from the things of the spirit practicing daily the requirement of his righteousness, which can only lead to fruitfulness. Moreover, our thoughts must be in agreement to the point whereby it is totally dominated by the things of the Spirit. If not we will continue to remain unfruitful knowing that the thoughts that is in hostility with the spirit cannot prosper or find any peace. Understand this therefore, if we do not possess and exercise the God-kind of response in our trials, adversities and circumstances, we will fail to produce the right kind of fruits that will bring glory to the Kingdom of God. Now let us continue the journey of liberation from the unfruitful deeds of bondage as we direct our attention to this portion of scripture while allowing our minds to be governed by the Spirit. Romans 8:4-8 NIV says,

'In order that the righteous requirement of the law might be fully met in us, who do not live according to the flesh but according to the Spirit. Those who live according to the flesh have their minds set on what the flesh desires; but those who live in accordance with the spirit have their minds set on what the spirit desires. The mind governed by the flesh is death but the flesh governed by the spirit is life and peace. The mind governed by the flesh is hostile to God; it does not submit to God's law, nor can it do so. Those who are in the realm of the flesh cannot please God.'

Unless the worldly thoughts of mankind truly experience real conversion, it will always keep us in constant conflict with our spirit, making us ineffective and unproductive in our knowledge of God and His promises. Understanding the process and experience that is associated with transformation is critical. Changing from one belief to another is not always easy, but the truth will set us free. Renewing one's thought will not occur with empty words, nor a feel-good speech. The vicious cycle of such ignorance that have been practiced for so many years only continues to lead you into an unprofitable lifestyle of frustration and unbelief. Obviously, by now, we should definitely recognize the genuine need for pursuing godly thoughts that would produce healthy results through righteous beliefs. Furthermore, the fact is, no one can truly change their lives until they have changed their unbelief and skepticism, especially when it comes to the subject of faith, for no one can rise above their thoughts. This is why it is necessary for you to enter into a covenant of agreement to seek God's thoughts wholeheartedly each day, faithfully making your commitment and sacrifice, energy and time to eagerly pursue and remove all ungodly thoughts from your life with honest intention and integrity. Then you will truly come to realize that your labor of sacrifice was not in vain and your commitment have richly rewarded you. And yes, the fruit never bears away from the tree, but in it, and on it for the world to see. Prudently now let us accept these gracious words from the Father of our spirit as is written in Jeremiah 29:11-13 KJV that says,

'For I know the thoughts that I think toward you, saith the Lord, thoughts of peace, and not of evil, to give you an expected end. Then shall ye call upon me, and ye shall go and pray unto me, and I will hearken unto you. And ye shall seek me, and find me, when ye shall search for me with all your heart.'

It's only during the process of seeking God for ourselves we will personally find Him, and receive our deliverance, joy, peace, wisdom and understanding. Miracles have a funny way of showing up in the moment of our darkest times and when we least expect it. Now according to the scripture, please notice that it did not say, it was when we hear the word of the Lord that we have found him, but it said, when we deliberately and wholeheartedly search for Him that we will find Him. Certainly, this gives us a clear indication that we have an obligation to perform. We must take action for change to come. Make no mistake about it, no one can fulfill your responsibility for you. Respectfully, every man must carry his own cross. What we can do, however, is to diligently encourage and strengthen each other along the way with comfort we have received from the Lord Jesus Christ. Remember, He is the Father of compassion, and He is willing and able to console and comfort us in all our troubles. It is, therefore, indicative to understand the true power and the driving force that is behind our most dominance pattern of thoughts because it is through our thoughts that we communicate what is our set plan of action, and also is revealed the secret motive of our hearts. For such cause I admonish you to give more careful consideration to your daily pattern of thoughts. Before you decide to act upon them, know that we do err by thoughts, words, and deeds. Consequently, we succeed by them likewise. For this reason, purging ourselves from wrong thinking should now become our ultimate priority immediately. Everyone must take their responsibility and start doing some deep personal soul searching by examining their thoughts and feeling to make any necessary correction that is needed to bring about quality improvement and success, is possible through your ways of living through the purest and highest standard of thinking you can possess.

Here are some treasured words from the mouth of God in Isaiah 55:6-9NIV that says, *'Seek the Lord while He may be found; and call on Him while He is near. Let the wicked forsake their ways and the unrighteous their thoughts. Let them turn to the Lord, and he will have mercy on them and to our God, for he will freely pardon. "For my thoughts are not your thoughts, neither are your ways my ways," declares the Lord. "As the heavens are higher than the earth, so are my ways higher than your ways and my thoughts than your thoughts."'*

Earnestly, if you have not been satisfied with the fruit that you are now harvesting and truly have the desire to do much better, then now is the season, and the perfect opportunity for you to start analyzing carefully the seeds that you have being planting throughout the years, not forgetting that our words are seeds. The problem is, have you been planting words of lies or of truth? When the seeds that we have sown are conceived and spring up in us, then they become fruit bearing trees living in our hearts. Oftentimes we do forget or even take for granted the creative reality, strength, and power of our words, undermining the fruit which they can and do produce in everyone's lives. When we use them inappropriately, they have a domino effect, which brings disaster. We cannot continue to ignore the negative impact they stir up within the human soul leading them into death and destruction, when they are not corrected early. There are lives to be saved. We must cultivate an awareness of how the Father of all creation feels, and see how He dealt with the inclination of evil thoughts from the beginning. It is recorded in Genesis 6:5-8 NIV that,

'The Lord saw how great man's wickedness on the earth had become on the earth, and that every inclination of the thoughts of his heart was only evil all the time. The Lord regretted that he had made human beings on the earth, and his heart was deeply troubled. So the Lord said, "I will wipe from the face of the earth the human race I have created – and with then the animals and creatures that move along the ground – for I regret that I have them." But Noah found favor in the eyes of the Lord.'

According to the substantial amount of evidence which has been revealed and confirmed through this portion of scripture reading, I hope and pray that the Word of God speak to your souls and also create in you a mighty spiritual awakening in your innermost being as you continue to allow the power of the Truth to surge deeply within your heart daily. By doing so, it will enhance your confidence to courageously come face to face with the spirit of the truth, accepting the that is more profitable to help people than to hurt or discourage them with negative words or deeds, fully knowing that your success is totally dependent upon your God given ability to think, speak, and do right while living upon the earth. Now developing a higher level of consciousness of one's own existing pattern of thoughts should become your primary focus so that you will be able to prevent the enemy form beguiling you through the use of his wiles. By doing so, you will no longer allow him to persuade, lead, trick, or outwit you into thinking, speaking or doing anything ungodly anymore. Knowing that his desire and responsibility is to corrupt your soul and cheat you out of your spiritual inheritance, should be an incentive, for you to speak and do right. He has always been deceiving people from the beginning of God's creation, having them practice principles of deception which only leads to fruitless deeds of darkness and emptiness. Satan veils the minds of his victims by burying their thoughts from the true reality of life with his concealing curtain of darkness and deception preventing them from having a zealous desire to know the full truth about God's promises hidden in Christ Jesus, predestined for their glory. The enemy, continues to oppress them with his lies to the point whereby they become unbelievers being fully despaired by life itself.

Now that your awareness have been heightened to the level where you understand the power of your thoughts, accepting the facts that your mind is the birth place of success or failure, and your adversary is planning your demise through the use of his deceptive principles of lies, and empty words of darkness. In spite of all this, know that there is HOPE. There is hope for everyone who believes in God's Holy words knowing that everybody makes mistakes and the truth is that they are correctable. For this reason God sent His Son to show us how to make the necessary correction in our lives. It's time to turn your life around with Godly principles that cannot return void by magnifying this mind producing portion of scripture from Philippians 4:6-9NIV that says,

"Do not be anxious about anything, but in every situation, by prayer and petition, with thanksgiving, present your requests to God. And the peace of God, which transcends all understanding, will guard your hearts and your minds in Christ Jesus. Finally, brothers and sisters, whatever is true, whatever is noble, whatever is right, whatever is pure, whatever is lovely, whatever is admirable – if anything is excellent or praiseworthy- think about such things. Whatever you have learned or received or heard from me or seen in me – put it into practice and the God of peace will be with you."

It's fully time for us to wake up and realize the truth that if a man cannot manage his mind then he is not able to manage his life, knowing that wherever the thoughts go, the action is right behind. You see, the strategy of Satan is that he desires praise, worship, and glory for himself through us. Unconsciously, many times we render such service to him through our negative thoughts, speech, and deeds. Yes indeed, by doing so, we are only helping the devil to rob, kill and destroy our very own lives. People who chase fantasies have no sense of reality in this world. They are trapped by their sinful thoughts and beliefs. One should be very careful then, how one goes about advertising their mistakes, and the injustices which others have done to them. Likewise, how they think and discuss the weaknesses of other people.

Here is another fruit producing scripture: Matthew 12:33-37 NIV says, *"Make a tree good and its fruit will be good, or make a tree bad and its fruit will be bad, for a tree is recognized by its fruits. You brood of vipers, how can you who are evil say anything good? For the mouth speaks what the heart is full of. A good man brings good things out of the good stored up in him, and an evil man brings evil things out of the evil stored up in him. But I tell you that everyone will have to give an account on the day of judgment for every empty word they have spoken. For by your words you will be acquitted, and by your words you will be condemned."*

Well, imagine if today was the Day of Judgment and you were standing before the Almighty God to give an account for every idle words, deceptive scheme, contrived plan or fabrication that you have spoken or used during your lifetime her on earth. How would you plead to the charge? Guilty or not guilty? If you were found guilty, at that moment what would your emotion be, knowing that this is it? You would have no one to plead for the wrong things you knew you were doing? Even worse, you rejected God and His guidance? Today, you have a chance, while you are still living. When your conscience should bothers you, or whenever you find yourself doing or saying something morally wrong to others, STOP, remember, this is an opportunity to do right. It's an opportunity for your words to acquit you at a crucial moment, and because you are aware, it's your responsibility to help others make it through the spiritual force of darkness and evil which exists in this world.

We cannot afford to be ignorant of Satan's schemes, of his systematic pattern of arranging how to beguile us. Let us put on, and wear daily our defensive cover of protection that we may take our stand against his schemes. The following portion of scripture wisely informs us of how we are to equip ourselves against the wiles of the enemy. Ephesians 6:10-19NIV says,

'Finally, be strong in the Lord and in His mighty power. Put on the full armor of God, so that you can take your stand against the devil's schemes. For our struggle is not against flesh and blood, but against the rulers, against the authorities against the powers of this dark world and against the spiritual forces of evil in the heavenly realms. Therefore, put on the full armor of God, so that when the day of evil comes, you may be able to stand your ground, and after you have done everything, to stand. Stand firm then, with the belt of truth buckled around your waist, with the breastplate of righteousness in place, and with your feet fitted with the readiness that come from the gospel of peace. In addition, to all this, take up the shield of faith, with which you can extinguish all the flaming arrow of the evil one. Take the helmet of salvation and the sword of the Spirit, which is the word of God. And pray in the spirit on all occasions with all kinds of prayers and requests. With this in mind, be alert and always keep on praying for all the Lord's people.'

Please be alert always and the wisdom of God will bless and save you forever.

8

Faith That Inspires One to Actions.

Without an inspired action from our faith it is impossible for anyone to please God. At time we may be deceived into thinking that we are pleasing others, or even ourselves, but unmistakably, millions of believers have misconstrued the true purpose and practicality of what genuine faith is about. They have not engaged themselves wholeheartedly in any steady course of action that consume their thoughts, time and energy applying the visionary principled thoughts of God into their daily quest for success. Well, just imagine how dangerous it is whenever a believer loses their spiritual sight of the institutional instruction and activities that is connected with the living word of faith, which is to render a service of care to a lost and dying world. Absolutely, it is futile for someone to profess that they believe intellectually God's word and yet, still without having any personal commitment to what they are confessing such faith is at the very least inadequate. Certainly, therefore, in order for a believer to move forward and become productive in their practice of faith, they need to reestablish a better foundational understanding of the knowledge of faith and duty because first of all, faith is not just hearing God's words and putting them into practice, but it is the spirit of the person Christ Jesus who came and dwelt on the inside of every believer who has accepted him as their personal Lord and Savior. Without the spirit of faith, it would be impossible for anyone to response to the things of God faithfully and wholeheartedly. Let us concentrate deeply within our hearts on these words which explains the concept of faith, from Hebrew 11:1-6 NIV that says,

'Now faith is the confidence in what we hope for and assurance about what we do not see. This is what the ancients were commended for. By faith we understand that the universe was formed at God's command, so that what is seen was not made out of what was visible. By faith Abel brought God a better offering than Cain did. By faith he was commended as righteous, when God spoke well of his offerings. And by faith Abel still speaks, even though he is dead. By faith Enoch was taken from this life, so that he did not experience death: "He could not be found, because God had taken him away." For before he was taken, he was commended as one who pleased God. And without faith it is impossible to please God, because anyone who comes to him must believe that he exists and that he rewards those who earnestly seek him.'

Whenever the head is removed from a thing the body will automatically die, so unless one is connected through Christ Jesus then everything else is in vain. It was on Calvary's cross that it was made possible for us to have a genuine connection with the spirit of faith. If not, we would still be bound and controlled by some external set of rules and principles taught by unspiritual minds. In addition, we should understand this truth that we can only come alive by being connected with Christ through faith and truly upon our acceptance of Him by whom the Father sent the Spirit of Faith to reside into our hearts.

Now that we have access with the Founder and Perfecter of our faith, receiving such ability we now can start the process of acquaintance getting to know Him internally, growing and developing a strong intimate relationship with each other. It is also vitally important that we learn to listen, establishing a genuine understanding of hearing the voice of the spirit of faith, because its only then we will be able to respond to what he is quickening in our spirit. Growing and maturing in the faith must become the ultimate desire of all Christian believers distinguishing a clear understanding between having faith in God and not just an object of things which they want from him. It's time for us to recognize the truth that God will not settle for our mere acknowledgement of Him.

Certainly, He wanted us to be transformed into his image and likeness, and yes, indeed, He has already predestined His glory to be revealed in us.

Let us now examine and meditate upon this potential faith building scripture passage from Matthew 17:16-21NIV that says,

> *"'I brought him to your disciples, but they could not heal him." "You unbelieving perverse generation," Jesus replied, "How long shall I stay with you? How long shall I put up with you? Bring the boy here to me." Jesus rebuked the demon, and it came out of the boy, and he was healed at that moment. Then the disciples came to Jesus in private and asked, "Why couldn't we drive it out?" He replied, "Because you have so little faith. Truly I tell you, if you have faith as small as a mustard seed you can say to this mountain, 'Move from here to there,' and it will move. Nothing will be impossible for you."'*

Now according to this portion of scripture reading, we understand that the faith of the disciples were very small when they started their relationship with Jesus, but the truth of the matter is this, every small seed of faith contain great potential of possibility living on the inside, a supernatural ability to grow and develop into something big. Knowing this, we should never despite small beginning again. Awaken to the truth that young faith needs to be nurtured and strengthened in the knowledge of God. Faith is more than just positive thinking, or expecting to receive a blessing from the Lord, but rather living a life transforming personality, and growing and developing an ever-increasing understanding of strength in the spirit of faith. It means confidently, trusting God to teach you to do the impossible things that unbelievers could only dream of doing. We understand, however, that the disciples had been given the authority to cast out demon and heal the sick, but unfortunately, at that time when they needed to heal the boy, their faith was undeveloped. They had not yet learned how to activate and exercise the power of their authority and likewise, you may find yourself in the same position right now, but be not discouraged and lean not on your own understanding, for this is your turning point. By accepting the truth that without the spirit of faith working in and through you it's just impossible to produce any kind of spiritual result, means that genuine faith will result in good works, and anyone who claims to have faith will be consistently inspired to live right by obeying God's command, and knowing that the evidence of being a believer is clearly demonstrated by their behavior of right action.

It is important, therefore, that we separate the fact from the fiction. Many people from all walks of life has been doing some good works but yet still, they do not have faith in the Lord Jesus Christ, while others claim to have faith in Him, and very rarely produce any form of good works. Their attitude and behavior hardly show forth any long-term vision of growth and development in the understanding of the power of faith. James 2:14-20 NIV tells us,

'What good is it, my brothers and sisters, if someone claims to have faith but has no deeds? Can such faith save them? Suppose a brother or a sister is without clothes and daily food. If one of you says them, "Go in peace; keep warm and well fed," but does nothing about their physical needs, what good is it? In the same way, faith by itself, if it is not accompanied by action, is dead. But someone will say, "You have faith; I have deeds." Show me your faith without deeds, and I will show you my faith by my deeds. You believe that there is one God. Good! Even demons believe that–and shudder. You foolish person, do you want evidence that faith without deeds is useless?'

Personally, I strongly suggest that you read the entire passage to get a complete definitive view of someone being internally motivated by the living spirit of faith. It should automatically create an exciting interest within, full of energy, wisdom and eagerness in one's heart. A supernatural stirring that is vigorously encouraging them to take a leap of faith into action, demonstrating active obedience in accordance with the divine inspiration and revelation which they have been obtaining from the Holy Spirit, making one become confidentially hopeful and resting faithfully in His promises. In addition, accepting this dynamic movement of faith, will stir up and make alive your soul, and take full effect in your heart. It must be nurtured and maintained by your love for Jesus, focusing your attention on his faithful deeds of action at work in and through your life, daily transforming and liberating you both spiritually and physically. According to your willingness and active obedience in response to God's instruction will activate your faith to demonstrate and show forth your reflection of belief in Christ Jesus who is the pioneer of your faith, whom the Father expressed Himself in fully. For this reason it is wise for every believer to take their responsibility seriously and make sure that their confidence, trust and reliance is totally built on the solid foundation of knowing Jesus Christ for themselves.

Respectfully now, let us carefully look over the story of the faith of the centurion in Luke 7:3-10NIV that says,

> 'The centurion heard of Jesus and sent some elders of the Jews to him, asking him to come and heal his servant. When they came to Jesus, they pleaded earnestly with him. "This man deserves to have you do this, because he loves our nation and has built our synagogue." So Jesus went with them. He was not far from the house when the centurion sent friends to say to him: "Lord don't trouble yourself, for I do not deserve to have you come under my roof. That is why I did not even consider myself worthy to come to you. But say the word, and my servant will be healed. For I myself am a man under authority with soldiers under me. I tell this one, 'Go' and he goes; and to that one, 'Come,' and he comes. I say to my servant, 'Do this,' and he does it." When Jesus heard this, He was amazed at him, and turning to the crowd following Him, He said, "I tell you I have not found such great faith even in Israel." Then the men who had been sent returned to the house and found the servant well.'

Now, there are seven qualities of life's lessons we all can learn from the Roman Centurion's demonstration of faith in this chapter.

1) He loves his people.
2) He built them a place of worship
3) He was a humble man
4) He believed in the positive result of his servant's healing even before Jesus spoke the word to him.
5) He respected the power of Jesus' authority
6) He understood the importance carrying out orders
7) He knew that Jesus did not need to be present in order for his servant to be healed.

The Power Of The Carpenter's Tool

Indeed, the centurion military officer, certainly did not allow his position, background, pride or any obstacles stand in his way from seeking help from the Lord Jesus Christ for his servant. Today, we have the opportunity to make the same determination of faith declaring that we will not allow any barriers to prevent us from getting the help which we are seeking from the Lord, who is commander in chief of Heaven and Earth. He holds the supreme answer to our faith, even the area where you may be in the practicing of your faith. He can help you with your struggles with self-doubts, fear, panic, unbelief, guilt or even with the scars of life. "But fear not" spiritually, I am here to announce to you in the mighty name of Jesus that your past is over. God is getting you ready to move you beyond yesterday's obstacles, and to bring you to the place of gestation where the spirit of faith is conceived in your soul, and gradually growing and developing in your mind. This shy faith is more than just positive thinking, it must be quickened before it comes alive. Now you are ready to accelerate in your action of faith, into having genuine trust, an inner confidence and loyalty to God, believing in the power of the secret knowledge of the Holy Spirit which God has deposited and revealed to your heart. Having your understanding sharpened daily to the secret knowledge and power of Jesus Christ, will automatically quicken your faith to the point where it comes to life. It is absolutely necessary for a believer to enter into such a phase before they can truly experience a living and active faith. All members of the household of faith must go through the process of reaching the stage of gestation, because this is the only place where authentic faith is conceived, grown and developed. What an awesome privilege and opportunity God has given to his people whereby He has made it possible for His children to bear and carry the gift of His Spirit. Confirm now and conform to the authentic birth of your faith in Christ Jesus. This is the key to your transformation into His image and likeness, granting you a prevailing advantage over your adversary, and the obstacles which were blocking your faith from moving mountains. Therefore, since God's new life has been born in us believers, we have the unction to function responsibly in the anointing of the spirit of faith hearing and communicating the truth of God's word effectively and producing good fruit.

Please give careful thoughts to this portion of scripture from Ephesians 6:10-17 NIV that says,

'Finally, be strong in the Lord and in His mighty power. Put on the full armor of God, so that you can take your stand against the devil's schemes. For our struggle is not against flesh and blood, but against the rulers, against the authorities, against the powers of this dark world and against the spiritual forces of evil in the heavenly realms. Therefore, put on the full armor of God, so that when the day of evil comes, you may be able to stand your ground, and after you have done everything, to stand. Stand firm then, with the belt of truth buckled around your waist, with the breastplate of righteousness in place, and with your feet fitted with the readiness that comes from the gospel of peace. In addition to all this, take up the shield of faith, with which you can extinguish all the flaming arrows of the evil one. Take the helmet of salvation and the sword of the Spirit, which is the Word of God.'

In order for you to stand your ground against the devil's schemes, you must learn to depend on God's faith to strengthen you so that you can skillfully use every piece of His armor to battle against the rulers of darkness in this world knowing that Satan fights believers deliberately with deception, and sometimes his lies seem like definite truth, but they are not! Strategically, he attacks the mind to create doubts and confusion, whereby one does not understand what is happening, or does not grasp the purpose of one's being, and the enemy uses this to destroy such a person. For this reason, it is not enough anymore for Christians to just know what God wants them to do, but rather demonstrate beliefs by their actions, which will reflect their faith, morally allowing the name of our Lord Jesus Christ and the deposit of the spirit of faith which has been given unto them be glorified in and through them throughout eternity. In addition, one should do their best to avoid the pitfall losing all the things which God as already preordained for them to achieve.

Wherever there is unbelief, there is danger as we read in Romans 9:30-33 NIV which says,

'What then shall we say? That the Gentiles who did not pursue righteousness, have obtained it, a righteousness that is by faith; by the people of Israel, who pursued the law as the way of righteousness, have not attained their goal. Why not? Because they pursued it not by faith but as if it were by works. They stumbled over the stumbling stone. As it

is written, "See, I lay in Zion a stone that causes people to stumble and a rock that makes them fall, and the one who believes in him will never be put to shame."'

According to this dynamic portion of scripture, it is severely critical for believers, as well as unbelievers to see that pursuing career jobs, goals, dreams and visions or even trying to achieve something for the kingdom without the spirit of faith, is destined to fail. This is why millions of God's chosen people are stumbling, they are not attaining, nor seeing the real fulfillment of their spiritual inheritance manifest in reality because they are not yet living their lives by quickening and indwelling power of Jesus Christ, who is the living word of our faith. It, therefore, has been a huge mistake for an individual to underestimate God's power of faith. Definitely, know that knowledge and understanding of the scriptures must take immediate effect on one's thoughts and vision, concerning oneself, about the present time and future. Acccepting the truth that there is liberating power in the word of the spirit of faith. The better we get to know about Christ's spirit of faith, the better it works within us and the greater our trust and confidence will be growing and increasing to a level high, whereby it will produce effective results.

Having a firm and upright belief in the spiritual realities and moral principles of the scriptural narrative and teaching should be viewed and accepted as God's favor fully extended to mankind through Christ. Therefore, one must willfully decide in his or her own heart to stick firmly to the adhering promises and agreements, faithfully exercising the powerful principles and authority of his words without wavering. We must be consciously alert of the fact that the evidence of the spirit of our faith must be clearly seen through our action, daily demonstrating compassion and love toward mankind and God. This is walking in the footsteps of the Master. In addition to all this, let us carefully examine this beautiful illustration of faith in action –the healing of a man in Acts 14:8-11NIV.

'In Lystra there sat a man who was lame. He had been that way from birth and never walked. He listened to Paul as he was speaking. Paul looked directly at him, saw that he had faith to be healed and called out, "Stand up on your feet!" At that the man jumped up and began

to walk. When the crowd saw what Paul had done, they shouted in the Lyconian language, "The gods have come down to us in human form!"

Finally, I hope and pray that these truth bring you lots of spiritual refreshment believing in your heart that a right understanding of the spirit of faith in Christ Jesus is definitely the key to producing maximum results of an unshakeable trust and confidence in relationship with God, practicing daily, active obedience to the spirit word of faith.

9

Called to Embrace The Sound Wisdom of God:

Beyond a shadow of a doubt the Bible calls for mankind to embrace and obey the wisdom of Almighty God. The doctrine of God's wisdom is trustworthy and flawless, free from blemish, defect, and errors. Definitely, it is explosive, powerful and effective, having a lot of power, strength and force to produce result in one's lives or circumstances, but for someone to really receive the benefit and understanding and the truth about God' wisdom, they must first study His words and ask Him to quicken it as a living reality into their spirit. They must also fully put those revealing truth into practice with all diligence of obedience and perseverance. For one must realize that all doctrine of teaching remain only a lifeless theory until it is quickened in their hearts and literally put into practice, for faith without works is dead. Furthermore, no matter how true or how scriptural a teaching may be, it does not have much effect on one's life unless it is obeyed. Indeed, whenever, it is quickened within the spirit of a person, it will cause them to come alive, and then show forth signs of life just like a fetus in the womb of a pregnant woman conceived with a child. As time goes by swiftly, the pregnancy starts to accelerate rapidly with growth and movement ready to manifest itself into the physical world.

Doubters from all walks of life refuse to listen and obey the sound and valuable doctrine of wisdom which comes straight from God's mouth, which is able to nourish, protect, and keep them from stumbling.

An offer of advice on every imaginable area of life that leads to fulfillment and contentment that one could ever dream of, but when they ignore his counsel, a professional guidance, this only leads to disappointments and disasters. This means safeguard your individual thought and behavior from all possible dangers and problems. Proverbs 1:20-22 NIV shows that wisdom is there for all, but when ignored serious problems arise.

'Out in the open wisdom calls aloud, she raises her voice in the public square; on top of the wall she cries out, at the city gate she makes her speech: "How long will you who are simple love your simple ways? How long will mockers delight in mockery and fools hate knowledge?"'

When seeming disaster strikes the disobedient unexpectedly, and they realize that they are eating the fruit of their foolish ways, which, is filled with the harvest of their contrived schemes influenced by the devil, the prince and ruler of darkness, truly then, they will come to their senses realizing the truth how their hearts have spurned correction. The teaching principles of the Almighty God, is able to make them wise. One has to realize that God's love is readily available to them, even in their sinful state. It is for this reason Christ died, and wisdom is made available for anyone willing to receive God's love, so whenever anyone acknowledges their transgressions, and repent at His rebuke, and ask for His forgiveness and mercy, His Love will help them to obey His command. Yes indeed, He will show and teach them wisdom from His secret place. Likewise, He will discipline and deliver them from all lifeless theory, and fill them with His promise, the abundant life which He has placed in Christ Jesus.

Now preparing to seek and follow His command, one should do their best not to become like the Pharisees, who diligently studied the scriptures, yet they did not receive a divine impartation of the life giving and quickening spirit. As you now focus your attention upon this portion of reading, John 5:36-40 NIV that says,

"I have testimony weightier than that of John. For the works that the Father has given me to finish–the very works that I am doing – testify that the Father has sent Me. And the Father who sent me has Himself testified concerning Me. You have never heard His voice nor seen His form, nor does His Word dwell in you, for you do not believe

the one He sent. You study the scriptures diligently because you think that in them you have eternal life. These are the very Scriptures that testify about me, yet you refuse to come to me to have life."

Now beloved, brothers and sister, make no mistake, it's all about Jesus Christ in the Word and beyond. He is the real Life Giver, Light and Resurrection of all human dead spirit, His assignment and responsibility is to bring back revival to the hearts and souls of His people, and I believe, even to this very day, He is still working in His Father's authority, reinstating everyone who will come to Him sincerely for life. He is restoring them back into the original position, which was forfeited by Adam, because of beguilement. Yes, gracefully, Jesus is resurging Believers daily back into their significant purpose, and they are performing meaningful duties and activities with a greater level of understanding of His righteousness. Friends, this experience comes through the process of an established relationship being born again, studying, growing, and developing in the true knowledge and revelation of God's secret wisdom hidden in Christ Jesus that was ordained for our glory before time began.

Let's acquaint ourselves with this powerful portion of scripture from 1 Corinthians 2:4-10NIV:

'My message and my preaching were not with wise persuasive words, but with a demonstration of the Spirit's power, so that your faith might not rest on human wisdom, but on God's power. We do, however, speak a message of wisdom among the mature, but not the wisdom of this age or of the rulers of this age, who are coming to nothing. No, we declare God's wisdom, a mystery that has been hidden and that God destined for our glory before time began. None of the rulers of this age understood it, for if they had, they would not have crucified the Lord of glory. However, as it is written: "What no eye has seen, what no ear has heard, and what no mind has conceived"—the things God has prepared for those who love him—these are the things God has revealed to us by His Spirit. The Spirit searches all things, even the deep things of God.'

Immediately, here and now, one must enroll themselves into the school of wisdom of the Holy Spirit, which is hidden in Christ Jesus. Acknowledging the truth that He is the secret treasure of Heaven sent by the Father to rescue those who will trust in His knowledge and put it into practice. He is the Deliverer you should be looking for, and need to know. Make yourself available, therefore, to Him and invest quality time searching wholeheartedly, for Him throughout the word so that you can get to know Him better and better each day. Furthermore, seeking God's wisdom may just turn out to be the most important decision you have ever made, and while you are on your journey pursuing His wisdom and understanding, you must try your very best to avoid all possible pitfall that will come and challenge your faith. Don't let anything become priority over your quest for God's wisdom. Likewise, you should no longer be wise in your own eyes, nor trust in your ideas, or lean on your vain imagination. Remember that the Holy Spirit is your perfect Teacher, and He knows how to educate and transform your life, and richly reward you according to your ability to obey His instruction. Bear in mind that nothing you desire in life can compare with what God's wisdom can produce for you.

Now allow your spirit to be illuminated with this passage of scripture from Proverbs 8:17-22 NIV that says,

'I love those who love me, and those who seek me find me. With me are riches and honor, enduring wealth and prosperity. My fruit is better than fine gold; what I yield surpasses choice silver. I walk in the way of righteousness, along the paths of justice, bestowing a rich inheritance and those who love me and making their treasure full. "The Lord brought me forth as the first of His works, before His deeds of old."'

To get more insight on this portion of scripture, I strongly suggest that you read the entire chapter. When someone gains firmness of mind and willpower to pursue God's wisdom for their lives, primarily, they are setting up a magnificent foundation for life, to grasp the spiritual realities that are deeply seated in God's words known as revelation. A possession of such relevant knowledge enables and strengthens one's ability to discern and makes wise choices and decisions in all practical matters, because the person is no longer leaning on his or her own understanding anymore, but rather on the divine intelligence of the Holy Spirit, to guide them along the way. Therefore, achieving a higher level of intelligence should always be our ultimate goal in life. To obtain the ability to apply one's knowledge appropriately and succeed in one's environment will produce a great feeling of joy and happiness, developing a mental advantage of some basic eternal qualities that will empower you, both intellectually and practically. This is the key on how to succeed in life, by skillfully advancing through life's raging storms with the revelation taught to you by the Holy Spirit. Moreover, as you continue to recognize that God is filling you with His Spirit, knowledge, wisdom and understanding, and skills to transform every aspect of your life, which will produce an unusual quality within you, cannot be denied.

It gives me great pleasure to direct your attention to these insightful and flawless words from Romans 16:25-27 NIV that says,

'Now to him who is able to establish you in accordance with my gospel, the message I proclaim about Jesus Christ, in keeping with the revelation of the mystery hidden for long ages past, but now revealed and made known through the prophetic writings by the command of the eternal God, so that all Gentiles might come to the obedience that comes from faith – to the only wise God be glory forever through Jesus Christ! Amen.'

Just focusing on the convincing evidence that is affirmed in the living word of God, should inspire you with a feeling of hopefulness, strongly believing in your heart that God is capable of giving you a supernatural ability to govern and discipline yourself, and to help others along the way. Through the revealing resources and usage of His wisdom, you can manage and succeed on all levels of life's affairs with sound judgment and practical skills. If you have the courage to imagine yourself in that position right now, then you can start performing it with a simple interest of faith by studying, believing and exercising the sound principles that is in the word of God. Surely this must be done consistently, always showing steady conformity of belief and action without any contradiction, knowing that a man's skills is manifested in his/her work. If there's no consistency in the way that he/she applies himself in the teaching wisdom of God, then he/she will not see the proper result which he desires. Therefore, be not intoxicated with the follies of this world any longer that can so easily contaminate the precious spirit and minds of individuals who lack prudence causing them to destroy their future through the practicing of foolish and unprofitable activities that lead them into poverty, prison or death. Nevertheless, God's wisdom is designed to console, deliver, protect and transform them from the unfruitful deeds of darkness and disappointment. His consolation is guaranteed to help them to counteract and overcome all the follies this world has to offer.

Certainly, this can only manifest through their cooperation, and consistent discipline, and practical usage of God's teaching. Deeply engage your mind now, and carefully evaluate these wise saying from Ecclesiastes 9:13 – 18 NIV which says,

'I also saw under the sun this example of wisdom that greatly impressed me: There was once a small city with only a few people in it. And a powerful king came against it, surrounded it and built huge siege works against it. Now there lived in that city a man poor but wise, and he saved the city by his wisdom. But nobody remembered that poor man. So I said, "Wisdom is better than strength." But the poor man's wisdom is despised, and his words are no longer heeded. The quiet words of the wise are more to be heeded than the shouts of a ruler of fools. Wisdom is better than weapons of war, but one sinner destroy much good.'

Yes, surely indeed, as you continue to reflect upon the amazing power that comes through God's wisdom, you can see it is far more profitable than all asset of human's strength put together. Likewise, it is also greater than any massive amount of weapons one could ever use in military warfare. Yet still, in today's society, people are gravitating vigorously toward material possessions, seeking to honor success and wealth above the wisdom of God. The truth about His intelligence is unrecognized. It has become unacceptable to the masses of people in the world. Even though it is the most powerful and effective substance which cannot be repealed or returned void, yet it is also widely ignored. If only they knew the exceptional qualities and ability that God's wisdom will produce in them, they would start esteeming the words of His mouth right now more than even the physical food which they eat, and above the material possessions they are trying so hard to achieve daily.

It is, therefore, critical for one to understand that there are two kinds of wisdom that is at work in the world. One is earthly and demonic; the other is supernatural and superior, which surpasses the earthly merits in qualities beyond the visible universe. Deliberately now, apply your heart and mind to comprehend this portion of scripture from James 3:13-18 NIV which says,

'Who is wise and understanding among you? Let them show it by their good life, by deeds done in the humility that comes from wisdom. But if you harbor bitter envy and selfish ambition in your hearts, do not boast about it or deny the truth. Such "WISDOM" does not come down from Heaven but is earthly, unspiritual, and demonic. For where you have envy and selfish ambition, there you find disorder and every evil practice. But the wisdom that comes from heaven is first of all pure; then peace-loving, considerate, submissive, full of mercy and good fruit, impartial and sincere. Peacemakers who sow in peace reap a harvest of righteousness.'

Here we can clearly see that there are two different kinds of wisdom, both of which, yield different results. When we practice using the instruction learned through God's words, the secret of developing and conducting oneself in a prevailing manner becomes evident. We experience peace, and we become loving, considerate, impartial, and full of mercy and sincerity. When someone obtains the power of distinguishing the truth and they're able to separate fact from fiction because of the customary usage of God's wisdom, they will put an end to their unsuccessful practice of all vain traditions. This will release them from the world's seductive attractions because they will discover for themselves that there are no substitutes for what God's wisdom is offering them.

Let's energetically now focus on these words from Proverbs 3:13-19 NIV that says,

'Blessed are those who find wisdom, those who gain understanding, for she is more profitable than silver and yields better returns than gold. She is more precious than rubies; nothing you desire can compare with her. Long life is in her right hand; in her left hand are riches and honor. Her ways are pleasant ways, and all her paths are peace. She is a tree of life to those who take hold of her; those who hold her fast will be blessed. By wisdom the Lord laid the earth's foundations, by understanding he set the heaven in place;'

When you are pursuing good success both physically and spiritually you must emancipate yourself from all meaningless talk and deception, socially and politically. Yes indeed, from all traditional rules of men that only limits what you can do, and hold firm to the trustworthiness of the message of the cross of Jesus, because it is the power of God that brings salvation to everyone who believe. Understanding the grace of God, means daily practicing and using the soundness of His wisdom, which cannot be resisted or contradicted when it is used appropriately in every circumstance of life. Consciously, your primary focus must be totally set upon the wisdom of God for insight, whereby you prepare daily to listen and obey all his instruction in season and out of season whether you feel like it or not. You must practice using His words effectively to the point whereby it produces result. Definitely, it is your passport and authorized identification for success knowing that God promised that His words will not return void, and you can trust that God does keep His word.

Let's concentrate on this powerful portion of scripture from Isaiah 55:7-11 KJV that says,

'Let the wicked forsake his way, and the unrighteous man his thoughts: and let him return unto the Lord, and he will have mercy upon him; and to our God, for he will abundantly pardon. For my thoughts are not your thoughts neither are your ways my ways, saith the Lord. Far as the heavens are higher than the earth, so are my ways higher than your ways, and my thoughts than your thoughts. For as the rain cometh down and the snow from heaven, and returneth not thither, but watereth the earth, and maketh it bring forth and bud, that it may give seed to the sower, and bread to the eater: So shall my word be that goeth forth out of my mouth: It shall not return unto me void, but it shall accomplish that which I please, and it shall prosper in the thing whereto I sent it.'

Now, according to this passage of scripture, we recognize the truth that God accomplishes and achieves His desire through the usage of His powerful words, which He has sent out on a mission to rescue, heal and save the hearts and souls of everyone who is willing to listen and obey His counsel. They shall experience the credible evidence of reality, which comes from His wisdom working from generation to generations.

The Power Of The Carpenter's Tool

No believer, therefore, should remain unskillful, ineffective and unproductive in their faith anymore. We who are Christians today are the true and blessed heirs of God's knowledge and wisdom on the earth dispelling the darkness that surrounds the world, because of the Holy Spirit that dwells within us. The more we know Him, the more we can appreciate what He has done for us. In fact, we are grateful to God for His personal concern, help and mercy toward us. His creation provides everything we need when we apply His wisdom to our lives and circumstances. Understanding the usage and benefits we get from using God's wisdom is the master key to one's salvation and prosperity in this life and the one to come.

Meditate on these words from Proverbs 16: 20-25 NIV that says,

"Whoever gives heed to instruction prospers, and blessed is he who trusts in the Lord. The wise in heart are called discerning, and pleasant words promote instructions. Understanding is a fountain of life to those who have it, but folly brings punishment to fools. A wise man's heart guides mouth, and his lips promote instruction. Pleasant words are a honeycomb, sweet to the soul and healing to the bones. There is a way that seems right to a man, but in the end it leads to death."

Now, remember that God is sovereign over every situation. He is all powerful. He always acts at the right time.

10

The Assignment of Your Words.

Giving your words an assignment is a master key that leads to great achievements in life. As the light of illumination and inspiration leaps into your spirit causing powerful truths to become a living and enduring reality to you, you are forced to start taking immediate responsibility for each word that will proceed out of your mouth from this day forth and forever. Now, from the beginning of creation we recognize this powerful and miraculous truth that God gave His words an assignment to do something and it produced the results which He desired. This is recorded in Genesis 1:3, 6, 9, 11, 14 20, 24, 26 and 29, for us to read. It tells us, *'God said, "Let there be," and there was.'* Something happened. He spoke very effectively and concisely and His words produced results. There is no doubt that God's word contains invisible power. This is why our relationship with Him is an absolute necessity. Remember that it is, **'The Spirit of God hath made me, and the breath of the Almighty hath given me life.'** (Job 33:4) NIV

God's words are the blueprint written in our hearts, guiding us into our daily assignment to overcome ignorance, poverty, darkness, sickness and the diseases of this world. Now the question is: Are you ready to be fully in partnership with God and His words? Will you faithfully believe in the message of the cross? If your answer is yes, then start practicing using it as an occupational therapy, expecting it to produce results for you and those you will come in contact with. Avail yourself to understand the way in which spiritual words are used will drastically place you in a position of authority, power and strength. Learning to make better usage of God's word is a master key to gain advantage over your enemies and life's circumstances. In fact, Proverbs 24:5-7 NIV tells us that:

'The wise prevail through great power, and those who have knowledge muster their strength. Surely you need guidance to wage war, and victory is won through many advisers. Wisdom is too high for fools; in the assembly at the gate they must not open their mouths.'

When you have something and don't know the true value of it, or how to use it appropriately, then it will become unimportant and unproductive to you. Today, however, is the beginning of your turning point. To walk away from the empty way of life, and say enough is enough, even though you have gone through the season of unrelenting pain and suffering, but you should never deny the words of the Holy One. Remember His words has power to heal and deliver you from the cruel and unfair world system. Give special attention to these words from Psalm 107:19-21NIV that tells us,

'Then they cried to the Lord in their trouble, and he saved them from their distress. He sent out His word and healed them; He rescued them from the grave. Let the give thanks to the Lord for His unfailing love and His wonderful deeds for mankind.'

Convincingly, I believe that God's words has mental skills and powers to rescue and prosper anyone who will believe it, and have the audacity to put them into practice (usage) knowing that success comes by accessing both mental and physical skills. When they are in harmony, success is definite. When one is able to use their intelligence and physical strength to do something on a high level of proficiency then they will become unstoppable. To get to this level, however, one must first overcome the warfare that lie silently within themselves known as the logic of the mind, and activate the faith of the heart. These two constantly oppose each other. Intense warfare will always emerge whenever you are in pursuit of your freedom spiritually, physically, and financially. However, if you can discipline your mind to unite and come into agreement with the knowledge of faith in the heart, then half the battle is already won. Strategically, therefore, clothe yourself mentally with the whole armor of God, recognizing that in the true reality of life that success cannot be obtained by depending upon the strength of the flesh alone. Concentrate on these words from Hosea 4:6 NIV and see what I mean. It says,

'My people are destroyed from lack of knowledge. "Because you have rejected knowledge, I also reject you as my priests; because you have ignored the law of your God, I also will ignore your children."'

We must give careful thoughts to the cause and effect of our words. Certainly, millions around the world are suffering blows from the mouth of the enemy physically, spiritually, and economically, because of their disobedience and unbelief and deliberate refusal to surrender and do what God has told them to do. When they humble themselves, however, and start obeying His teaching, He will shorten any lengthy season of struggling which they were encountering. Submitting to God's authority, therefore, and learning to control one's tongue is the ultimate goal to reduce damage and destruction to oneself and others. Everyone is responsible, and will be held accountable for how they use what they fully know. They are aware that their words have effect on others. Wrongfully using our tongue to gossip, slander, manipulating and putting others down is immoral. Immediately, start making arrangement to bridle your tongue before you speak another word, ask yourself this question: Is what I am about to say, kind? Is it going to produce the kind of harvest I truly desire? Being conscious of the fact that Satan uses the tongue to divide and destroy relationships, causing people to be against one another leaving lives with lasting scars and pain, but the Lord will send deliverance to them who will stand their ground in His words by concentrating on their commitment and relationship with Him. Meditate also on this powerful portion of scripture from James 3:1-6 NIV that says,

'Not many of you should become teachers, my fellow believers, because you know that we who teach will be judged more strictly. We all stumble in many ways. Anyone who is never at fault in what they say is perfect, able to keep their whole body in check. When we put bits into the mouths of horses to make them obey us, we can turn the whole animal. Or take ships as an example. Although they are so large and are

driven by strong winds, they are steered by a very small rudder wherever the pilot wants to go. Likewise, the tongue is a small part of the body, but it makes great boasts. Consider what a great forest is set on fire by a small spark. The tongue also is a fire, a world of evil among the parts of the body. It corrupts the whole body, sets the whole course of one's life on fire, and is itself set on fire by hell.'

According to this portion of scripture, you acknowledge the truth that you can steer your life by the discipline of your tongue into the direction of success or destruction. Yes indeed, such bill of rights is in the power of your hands, and the choice is yours to use wisely. Having one's heart filled with God's Holy words will automatically help to change the remaining course of their lives, because out of the abundance of one's heart the mouth speaks. There are only two things we all can achieve from our words. One is blessing. The other is condemnation. From blessings we get acceptance, from condemnation, we get disapproval. This is the result of what a man's speech will produce for him. All successful people understand the benefits of controlling their tongue, they know what to say, and how to say it in a manner whereby it produces effective results for them. Ponder within your heart the question, what are my words producing for me? Or how can I start using my words carefully and skillfully whereby it produces effective results for me?

Here in Mark 11:20-25 NIV we see the powerful effects of one's words. In this case Jesus' words. It reads:

'In the morning as they went along, they saw the fig tree withered from the roots. Peter remembered and said to Jesus, "Rabbi, look! The fig tree you cursed has withered!" "Have faith in God," Jesus answered. "Truly I tell you, if anyone says to this mountain, 'Go throw yourself into the sea,' and not doubt in their heart but believes that what they says will happen, it will be done for them. Therefore I tell you, whatever you ask for in prayer, believe that you have received it, and it will be yours. And when you stand praying, if you hold anything against anyone, forgive them, so that your Father in heaven may forgive you your sins."'

After reading and seeing the big picture of God's love and compassion, you realize that no one is beyond redemption. Having faith to believe in God's words is the beginning of one's recovery from all illnesses, spiritually, physically, socially, and financially. All believers must, therefore, establish an immovable foundation of faith for themselves through the supervision and guidance of God's wisdom and knowledge which is the general source of strength and power that leads men on a stable pathway to victory and success. It is important, also, to understand that the profession and confession of your faith believing will demand that your life shows forth fruitful evidence. Likewise, it is in your best interest to learn how to highly esteem the words of God above fear and doubts because they will automatically disqualify all expectation of receiving your heart's desire. Today, start planning tomorrow's triumphs because you are no longer journeying into yesterday's failure considering that your past is over as you begin to supernaturally immerse yourself into the ability, strength and power of God's Holy words. By totally investing in His wisdom to become informed, developed and matured, you will confidently portray a skillful attitude, understanding the usage and purpose of the gospel message of the cross by correctly handling and following its instruction daily. Suddenly you will come to realize the reality and truth that whenever you follow His words, you are allowing the Holy Spirit to steer your life into a destiny greater than what you could have ever chosen, planned, dreamed or imagined for yourself.

Everyone who believes God should start adapting and applying themselves to be led by the Holy Spirit, who is able to transform and transition their lives out of the evil forces of darkness, and place them into the abundant life which God has promised. Now know that all things are possible for us because of the atoning Blood of Jesus Christ, who has corrected our relationship with God the Father of creation once and for all, by dying on the cross and taking away our sins, thereby giving us access by the spirit of faith to discern the purpose of every conversation to see whether or not they are coming from a pure heart, or evil intent. Acquaint now yourself with these words from Matthew 12:33-37 KJV and see how it applies to our conversations producing evil or good results. It says, *"Either make the tree good, and his fruit good; or else make the tree corrupt; and his fruit corrupt: For the tree is known by his fruit. O generation of vipers, how can ye being evil, speak good things? For out of the abundance of the heart the mouth speaketh. A good man out of the good treasure of the heart bringeth forth good things: And an evil man out of the evil treasure bringeth forth evil things. But I say unto you, that every idle word that men shall speak, they shall give account thereof in the day of judgment. For by thy words thou shalt be justified and by thy words thou shalt be condemned."*

This portion of scripture automatically put your into a personal soul searching position. Question start screaming loudly in your heart, asking you what are your words doing for you? Are they just careless and empty? Are they bearing fruit for you? Are they condemning you and others? Well quite frankly, we all are the first beneficiary of our words. Every ungodly conversation is like an invisible switchblade placed at your throat slowly killing you without leaving a scar. You are responsible for repairing your life through usage (practice) of the spirit and life of God's Holy words. Practice disciplining your lips to speak positive and uplifting words. You must always cultivate an atmosphere for the presence of God to reveal His glory in you. He wants to strengthen your faith to the point where your life reflect His beauty. Willfully, one must take God and His counsel seriously. It will force you to renounce and avoid any participation of evil communication both privately and publicly. The priority goal of all believers is to establish a good rapport with God and His people because both is essential for successful living. Understanding the truth that skillful communication, and the power of agreement are the Master's tools to build friendly and faithful relationships here on Earth, bringing back harmony into creation. The influential words of God has power to affect changes in people's lives and circumstance. In addition, when you believe, and use what He gives you, He will show up in any situation in miraculous ways you would not have dreamed of. So, be wise, start using today's privilege and transform tomorrow's circumstances. Please do not put your life's opportunity on hold any longer because sin has consequences and no one will get away with them forever.

Let's focus on this passage of scripture. Psalm 1:1-6 KJV that says,

'Blessed is the man that walketh not in the counsel of the ungodly, nor standeth in the way of sinners, nor sitteth in the seat of the scornful. But his delight is in the Law of the Lord; and in his law doth he meditate day and night. And he shall be like a tree planted by the rivers

of water, that bringeth forth his fruit in his season; his leaf also shall not wither; and whatsoever he doeth shall prosper. The ungodly are not so: But are like the chaff which the wind driveth away. Therefore, the ungodly shall not stand in the judgment, nor sinners in the congregation of the righteous. For the Lord knoweth the way of the righteous: But the way of the ungodly shall perish.'

Now what does it profit a man to spend his whole life seeking and hoping to achieve success with some ineffective and unproductive counseling? Surely, we know that some advice can be very credible meanwhile others can be critical and yes indeed everyman has a right to decide his own destiny. No one can make that choice for you. Whose instruction are you willing to follow? But before you make your decision, or if you have already decided, consider these question within your heart today:

Where did this advice that I am about to put my faith and trust in come from?

Where is it going to take me?

What will it produce for me?

The counseling you choose to listen and obey will determine the kind of future you will have. It also reveals your plan of action and behavior toward others. It reveals who is really controlling your destiny. It is, therefore, one's responsibility to seek out the truth before one makes any decision. This way they will be able to safeguard their thoughts against seducers, and imposters, who teach or give unprofitable counseling both naturally and spiritually. Nevertheless, one should understand that God's counseling stand sure forever. His word has been tried in a furnace and purified seven times. Yes, it has been put to the test throughout the ages.

Here's a lesson from the wise and foolish builders. Matthew 7:24-27 NIV which says,

"Therefore everyone who hears these words of mine and puts them into practice is like a wise man who built his house on the rock. The rain came down, the streams rose, and the winds blew and beat against that house; yet it did not fall, because it had its foundation on the rock. But everyone who hears these words of mine and does not put them into practice is like a foolish man who built his house on sand. The rain

came down, the streams rose, and the winds blew and beat against that house, and it fell with a great crash."

It is very important to know what God's word says, but it is far more profitable when we put it into practice using it to build our lives from generation to generation, knowing that God's words will guide us into a bright future in this present age and the one to come.

11

The Strength of Your Beliefs in God's Word:

Developing a strong and very courageous intellectual power through the great resources of God's wisdom is definitely the key to prove that you have gained confidence in the invisible and visible qualities of God's strength and power even before something literally becomes a reality to you. This supernatural strength that I am speaking about is beyond a person's physical power and energy, and no human words can describe or explain it in full details, because it can only be discerned through the moral force of faith. For someone to experience and demonstrate this spiritual strength of reality, they must first cultivate an hunger and thirst for God's righteousness by daily seeking to be nourished and strengthened with Divine revelation power from above. Bear in mind that this divine revelation is beyond one's normal capacity. It makes you intellectually rich through the soundness of God's faithful words. Being called and taught by the Holy Spirit of truth on receiving information of how to put off and deny your old self, which is your former conversations, and lives and practices, is a privilege available to all. The current revelation that God is inspiring them with, knowing that when their words can be backed up with actions, brings about a changed life-style.

Certainly, you know for sure that you are growing strong in the power of God's might, totally learning to trust and depend upon His strength which is available to us in Christ Jesus, who came to live in us by the Holy Spirit, demolishing the stronghold of our old futile mindset.

The Power Of The Carpenter's Tool

When we truly come in agreement wholeheartedly with Him, He will deliver us from all our weaknesses of character, and the futility of our thinking, which is vain, completely ineffective and useless. Following God's example of thinking, therefore, is the secret of resisting and overcoming the spiritual evil and weakness that plague the souls of man. Give careful thought to these words from Ephesians 4:17-19 NIV which says,

'So I tell you this, and insist on it in the Lord, that you must no longer live as the Gentiles do, in the futility of their thinking. They are darkened in their understanding and separated from the life of God because of the ignorance that is in them due to the hardening of their hearts. Having lost all sensitivity, they have given themselves over to sensuality so as to indulge in every kind of impurity, and they are full of greed.'

In accordance with this passage, would you agree that excessive pursuit for worldly pleasure has captured and preoccupied the minds and senses of millions of people, who are consistently seeking the gratification of the flesh above their spiritual needs? Lacking intellectual interest in the things of God, will allow one to become devoted to the influence of carnality. Indeed, they are blind and unable to see the things of God as of a greater value than the treasures of the world. Unfortunately, today, it seems like deficiency in moral values in society have become the normal way of life for most people. Certainly, they are unaware of the genuine purpose of the Holy Spirit, and how God sent His Son into the world to strategically redeem us from the curse and the empty ways of life. Instead, He adds values to our lives that we may grow strong in His wisdom daily becoming morally and spiritually fit. Respectfully, therefore, let me emphasize to you that the Holy Spirit is of greater value, so be not deceived anymore. Whenever a person receive the gift of the Holy Spirit in their hearts, He automatically increases their self-worth and begin a good work in them by educating them to become healthy, wealthy and wise through the knowledge of faith. Understanding the deposit of the Holy Spirit, is very important for one's growth and development. The deposit equips and empowers a person to utilize the supernatural strength of God to defend themselves and live a life pleasing unto Him. This tells us that God does not want us to live a defeated lifestyle. Recognizing this truth, why it is dangerous when someone's sensual desires overcome their spirituality and dedication to the Lord Jesus Christ? Such vain and deceptive philosophy is what causes mankind to lose their connection power and strength with God, who is more than able to direct their affairs of life. Concentrate carefully on this revealing portion of scripture from Hebrews 11:32-34 NIV and be strengthened. It says,

'And what more shall I say? I do not have time to tell about Gideon, Barak, Samson and Jephthah, about David and Samuel and the prophets, who through faith conquered kingdoms, administered justice, and gained what was promised; who shut the mouths of lions, quenched the fury of the flames, and escaped the edge of the sword; whose weakness was turned to strength; and who became powerful in battle and routed foreign armies.'

The inspiration that is now flowing gracefully in your heart is the strength of the Holy Spirit, reminding you that regardless of your past or the current disapproval of others toward you be not disheartened, God is your true source of real hope and confidence who is more than able to cause you to experience some outstanding victories. According to your faith, believe and be willing to obey His instruction, faithfully trusting that He will keep His promises to you even when you are feeling tired physically, and discouragement darken up your way, and you are trying to convince yourself that you cannot go another step further. Just remember that divine help is ready to place you into the supernatural realm demonstrating the truth that His strength is made perfect in your weakness. To discover such reality, can create a thrill of unspeakable joy and excitement that will surprisingly drive you to have and develop a greater level of interest in God. Remember that your ultimate desire is to gain a deeper level of spiritual understanding with Him through the power of His unfailing words. In addition, for one to build stamina/strength, and staying power in the faith. It will require spending quality time in the presence of God's Word studying daily, listening and doing what He is revealing and illuminating in your hearts. The more you get to know Him, the more you will appreciate what He's doing in and through you. Give prudence to the fact that His infinite value is better than your ways, because He is perpetually shedding everlasting light into your hearts relieving you from the temporal things. This will cause things that once were overvalued by you because of worldly opinions to change. You will develop quality strength of moral character guaranteed to help you make wise decisions raising you above life's distractions and difficulties.

It is imperative to understand values are most important to you: And now every believer should ask themselves this question. Does my actions reflect the world's values or God's values? Know that the strength of a man's beliefs is measured by how willing he is to suffer to see the manifest reality of those beliefs come to pass. Anchor your thoughts firmly on this portion of scripture from 2 Samuel 22:29-36 NIV that says,

'You, Lord, are my Lamp; The Lord turns my darkness into light. With your help I can advance against a troop; with my God I can scale a wall. "As for God, His way is perfect: The Lord's word is flawless; He shields all who take refuge in Him. For who is God besides the Lord? And who is the Rock except our God? It is God who arms me with strength and keeps my way secure. He makes my feet like the feet of the deer, He causes me to stand on the heights. He trains my hands for battle; my arms can bend a bow of bronze. You make your saving help my shield, your help has made me great."

Believe by faith that you receive strength, a supernatural power and energy that forces you into action and train you to persevere until you overcome and are able to withstand hardship, adversity, trial, and suffering. To persevere, one must develop an inward forceful ability continuously in their beliefs and action in the Lord, in spite of problems that comes to challenge them. Please understand adversity can be a very useful training tool in someone's life if they can perceive it in that light. Calculating the fact that your beliefs will be put to the test by the opposition which you are going to come face to face with and yes, indeed, when they show up they will reveal your weakness or strength – they will reveal who really are–the kind of character you have trained and developed into. Graciously, therefore, it is rewarding whenever a person spend quality time in God's presence, daily growing strong in the knowledge and understanding of His word. By fully trusting and obeying His counsel they will come to learn and view adverse circumstances as an opportunity whereby they can truly expect to experience God's faithfulness to manifest in those challenging situations of life. Furthermore, it is wise for someone to learn how to discipline themselves to rely on God's strength for their total effectiveness in all circumstances, rather than depending on their simple effort, energy, talents, and ability to overcome adversities knowing that it is so easy for someone to be deceived by the temporary benefits of wealth in the world. Obviously, all believers will undergo tremendous pressure of opposition once they have decided to live their lives the way God wants them to live, nevertheless, they must make up their mind to confront the unpleasant reality of adversities with calmness and confidence believing that God is in control of their destiny.

Magnify these words in your heart and gain inward strength to persevere. 2 Corinthians 1:5-10 NIV that says,

'For just as we share abundantly in the sufferings of Christ, so also our comfort abounds through Christ. If we are distressed, it is for your comfort and salvation; if we are comforted, it is for your comfort, which produces in you patient endurance of the same sufferings we suffer. And our hope for you is firm, because we know that just as you share in our sufferings, so also you share in our comfort. We do not want you to be uninformed, brothers and sisters, about the troubles we experienced in the province of Asia. We were under great pressure, for beyond our ability to endure, so that we despaired of life itself. Indeed, we felt we had received the sentence of death. But this happened that we might not rely on ourselves but on God, who raises the dead. He has delivered us from such a deadly peril, and he will deliver us again. On Him we have set our hope that He will continue to deliver us.'

The heartfelt inspiration that you are now receiving from the above reading is telling you that beyond a shadow of a doubt, you can overcome the haunting fear and feelings of inadequacy, and mental restriction of powerlessness which have been affecting your thoughts and producing a feeling of disqualification. This happens especially to those who depend on their own skills, abilities, and education, and not on God. They fail to believe that God's strength is their greatest source of power and it is sufficient to make them victorious in all trials and weakness. The proof of evidence that sustains a person claim of beliefs must be demonstrated by their action and not just by words only, because then they can faithfully accept the truth that God gave them the deposit of the Holy Spirit within their hearts by faith, whereby they can concentrate on Him internally to experience inner strength and power. They will become fearless.

In addition, it is imperative to meditate upon the historical records of the lives of the apostles, which reveals how sincere and unwavering they were in their beliefs and their commitment to that which was taught to them. Undoubtedly, they died for their faith in such a gruesome manner. The unimaginable bloodcurdling death which they died just because they were unwilling to deny their belief in Christ Jesus' resurrection, and that which they knew to be true. Therefore, they sealed their faith with their life's blood. Moreover, their unwavering and unrelenting claim of faith and conviction of belief is speaking volumes to our spirit, asking us modern day believers, what the true measurement of our belief in Christ Jesus is, and the message of the cross? This would only be wise and beneficial to us if we personalize, and ponder these two question deep within our hearts right now. What is the strength of my belief? And how can I measure the strength of my belief?

Well, according to the life of Jesus Christ, and the lives of the apostles, we are able to measure the strength of our beliefs by how much we are willing to stand up and suffer for righteousness for the truth we have accepted and hold dear to our hearts. Unfortunately, somehow we have swayed from such standard of principles and beliefs. For whenever some believers face certain adversities it becomes so easy for them to focus on the problem and the pain rather than on the spiritual goal, which is to follow in the footstep of the master, not allowing fatigue, pain, poverty, hardship, and criticism to force them off the pathway of life. But now, you can learn the genuine secret how to sustain your fellowship with Christ Jesus through the "Power of Love" as you internalize and personalize this strength. Draw and build confidently your faith with this portion of scripture from Romans 8:35-39 NIV that says,

'Who shall separate us from the love of Christ? Shall trouble or hardship or persecution or famine or nakedness or danger or sword? As it is written: "For your sake we face death all day long; we are considered as sheep to be slaughtered." No in all these things we are more than conquerors through Him who loved us. For I am convinced that neither death nor life, neither angels nor demons, neither the present nor the

future, nor any powers, neither height nor depth, nor anything else in all creation, will be able to separate us from the Love of God that is in Christ Jesus our Lord.'

Primarily, the first step in discovering and experiencing God's unconquerable love, grace and mercy in their lives, is to receive Jesus Christ, who is available to anyone who will accept His spiritual kingship. Then He will be able to fulfill the Father's promise in their lives baptizing them with the power of the Holy Spirit equipping them for their kingdom assignment. Certainly, then, they will understand the truth that belief is more than an intellectual agreement. It just cannot be forced to follow or accept, but rather is a direct willingness and determination that comes from the heart, resulting from the deposit of the Holy Spirit within making them become competent, which is an overwhelming assurance. Yes, indeed, a supernatural sufficiency of means to all life's requirements that makes one legally qualified capable and fit for success. Actually, having the deposit of the Holy Spirit living on the inside of a believer, is to have Jesus Himself, dwelling in their physical body, working for and with them. Therefore, begin to allow the spirit of God's strength, to start developing a strong spiritual personality within your heart and soul teaching you how to execute His wisdom and power in all opposition and adversities of life. Set your attention on these seven qualities that would make your relationship with Jesus Christ, a productive one. 2 Peter 1:3-11NIV says that,

'His divine power has given us everything we need for godly life through our knowledge of him who called us by His own glory and goodness. Through these He has given us His very great and precious promises, so that through them you may participate in the divine nature, having escaped the corruption in the world caused by evil desires. For this very reason, make every effort to add to your faith goodness, and to goodness knowledge; and to knowledge, self-control; and to self-control, perseverance, and to perseverance, godliness; and to godliness, mutual affection, and to mutual affection; love. For if you possess these qualities in increasing measures they will keep you from being ineffective and unproductive in your knowledge of our Lord Jesus Christ. But whoever does not have them is nearsighted and blind, forgetting that they have

been cleansed from their past sins. Therefore, my brothers and sisters, make every effort to confirm your calling and election. For if you do these things, you will never stumble, and you will receive a rich welcome into to the eternal kingdom of our Lord and Savior Jesus Christ.'

Now according to this inspired scripture reading, we recognize that faith is more than just belief in certain facts or positive thinking. Surely, it must result in action, which enhances Christian growth in character, and moral discipline. Today, we are privileged to belong to God's family, and certainly, everyone that is in this community is related to each other sharing the same values and interests, knowing that Christ is the founder and foundation of this great family. However, many believers would like to enjoy more of God's favor and kindness in their lives, but they are not willing to make sacrifice to get to know Him better through studying the Bible and prayer. In order for grace and peace to be multiplied in abundance, it will only come through the increasing of their knowledge of Him who calls them and empowers them by His divine nature. It is one's responsibility, therefore, to confirm their salvation, and faith in Christ Jesus, holding fast to the non-negotiable truth of His word believing that God's word is not just for their information, but rather for their transformation. Please give careful thought to this passage of scripture from Colossian 1:9-14 NIV which says,

'For this reason, since the day we heard about you, we have not stopped praying for you. We continually ask God to fill you with the knowledge of His will through all the wisdom and understanding that the spirit gives, so that you may live a life worthy of the Lord and please Him in every way: Bearing fruit in every good work, growing in the knowledge of God, being strengthened with all power according to His glorious might so that you may have great endurance and patience, and giving joyful thanks to the Father, who has qualified you to share in the inheritance of His holy people in the kingdom of light. For He has rescued us from the dominion of darkness and brought us into the kingdom of the Son He loves, in whom we have redemption, the forgiveness of sins.'

Finally my brothers, and sisters, be strong in the Lord Jesus Christ, for the most dangerous place for any human being to wake up and find themselves is to realize that the confidence that they once had in God has slipped away. Whereby, they are now depending upon human solution alone to solve their problems. This is why it is extremely important for me to warn and encourage every believer who is filled, and those who are seeking to be filled with the strength of God's spirit. that it is their personal responsibility each day to stay close to God, spending regular time with him in private discussion through daily Bible study and prayer, making His counsel your highest priority by putting into practice whatsoever secret things He reveals to you to do, and be patient for the result. Also, don't be discouraged when you feel like your faith in God is going unrewarded here on Earth, but consider this over carefully, that your greatest reward is not in this life, but in the life to come. Therefore, you must determine in your heart to make heaven your home. Continue to accept and appreciate the comfort and encouragement that you find in His presence knowing that we need to rely His strength for our success.

Meditate now upon these words from Isaiah 40:29-31 NIV that says,

'He gives strength to the weary and increases the power of the weak. Even youths grow tired and weary, and young men stumble and fall; but those who hope in the Lord will renew their strength. They will soar on wings like eagles; they will run and not grow weary, they will walk and not be faint.'

Remember that God does not only gives us His strength and power, for us to keep to ourselves, but He empowers us to demonstrate it in love to others.

12

The Power and Benefits of Making Inquiry.

Unfortunately, when someone has never done something before, or hasn't been in a position or place in their lives, and yet still they have a genuine passion to achieve those things, but constantly finding themselves coming up short and not being able to succeed because they do not have that particular experience, sufficient knowledge or skills which is required to accomplish those burning heartfelt desire and dreams, life can become overwhelmingly frustrated for such individuals. Well, just imagine carrying around such huge mental burden, an internal heaviness of failure resting in their souls. Definitely, it will cause a person to feel bad about themselves, thinking how ineffective and unproductive they are in their pursuit for fulfillment. The good news is this, there is hope, and there is a way out of darkness and ignorance. Yes, indeed, their minds can become unveiled by simply learning to see things from God's perspective. They must faithfully believe that the manufacturer is truly capable of repairing His product and make it become useful once again.

Let's concentrate on this conceivable portion of scripture from Hosea 4:6-7NIV that says,

'My people are destroyed from lack of knowledge. "Because you have rejected knowledge, I also reject you as my priest; because have ignored the laws of your God, I also will ignore your children. The more

the priests there were, the more they sinned against me; they exchanged their glorious God for something disgraceful."'

Now, one should bear in mind that God can and will use our negative experiences of failure. The defeated feelings that we are often burdened down with, He can use them to create one of the most precious moment of opportunity to reconcile us back to Himself. Therefore, if you are facing your desert right now, the valley of trials, problems, and temptations, just remember your Creator, the Sustainer of life, how He wants to bring you back into a personal relationship with Himself; developing an intimate level of communication, whereby you share your thoughts with Him, and in return receive divine revelation from Him that will totally refurbish your life. Your life will become wholesome again and you will recognize the truth that He provides inner healing and strength for the broken-hearted. This is why it is so important for every individual to create a God-consciousness awareness for themselves by centering their thoughts upon Him. Yes, by doing so one will start crowding out negative and wrong thinking.

God has given us an invitation to come and reason with Him, knowing that He holds the answer to our every need. For example, when Achan sinned, the Israelites military armed force got defeated at Ai, and Joshua, their leader went into the presence of the Lord and inquired about the situation. We will continue to read this powerful narrative in Joshua 7:6-12 NIV that says,

'Then Joshua tore his clothes and fell faced down to the ground before the ark of the Lord, remaining there till evening. The elders of Israel did the same, and sprinkled dust on their heads. And Joshua said, "Alas, Sovereign Lord, why did you ever bring this people across the Jordan to deliver us into the hands of the Amorites to destroy us? If only we had been content to stay on the other side of the Jordan! Pardon your servant Lord. What can I say, now that Israel has been routed by its enemies? The Canaanites and the other people of the country will hear about this and they will surround us and wipe out our name form the earth. What then will you do for your own great name?" The Lord said to Joshua, "Stand up! What are you doing down on your face? Israel has sinned; they violated my covenant, which I commanded them to

keep. They have taken some of the devoted things; they have stolen, they have lied, they have put them with their own possessions. That is why the Israelites cannot stand against their enemies; they turn their backs and run because they have made liable to destruction. I will not be with you anymore unless you destroy whatever among you is devoted to destruction."

Now according to this portion of the scripture, it clearly indicates to us that whenever a person's life plans fall short of the intended victory and glory that they are anticipating to come through, but never did, that God has to be consulted to find out what is amiss. Immediately, one should understand the truth that their setback is only a temporary delay, if they seize the opportunity quickly and apply exactly the same principles that Joshua and the elders did. They should go to God in deep humility and sorrow asking Him for forgiveness, help, and a new strategy of direction believing He is all-knowing and all-powerful, and His plan for our success cannot fail. We also learned about the awesome benefits that come through fasting and prayer. The moral of the story clearly revealed that God answers prayers. Whenever we seek His advice earnestly, this reminds us that we should always stay in God's presence pouring out our hearts to Him seriously sincerely not withholding anything from Him, because only God knows the truth about the things that lies ahead of us. Without a shadow of a doubt, we must believe that He can, and will reveal to us those secret things that are deeply hidden from us. If we diligently inquire of God, He will reveal the mystery to us. We see this in the life of King Nebuchadnezzar who had a dream that frightened him. He then summoned all his magicians, enchanters, sorcerers and astrologers to interpret his dream for him but unfortunately they could not, so he firmly decided and ordered the execution of all the wise men of Babylon. Daniel, however, went to the king and asked him for some time. So Daniel and his three friends went in the presence of God and pled for mercy. Let's read the scripture found in Daniel 2:17-23 NIV which says,

'Then Daniel returned to his house and explained the matter to his friends Hananiah, Mishael, and Azariah. He urged them to plead for mercy from the God of Heaven concerning this mystery, so that he and his friends might not be executed with the rest of the wise men of

Babylon. During the night the mystery was revealed to Daniel in a vision. Then Daniel praised the God of Heaven and said: "Praise be to the name of God for ever and ever; wisdom and power are his. He changes times and seasons; he deposes kings and raises up others. He gives wisdom to the wise and knowledge to the discerning. He reveals deep and hidden things; He knows what lies in darkness and light dwells with him. I thank and praise you, God of my ancestors: You have given me wisdom and power, you have made known to me what we asked of you, you have made known to us the dream of the king."'

According to these valuable life transforming principles which we are continuously discovering in the word of God, we believe that they are timeless, reliable and useful throughout all generation. Therefore, giving glory, praises and honor unto the Father, the God of Heaven and earth for revealing the greatest problem-solving strategy that He has kept in reserve for those who have established a personal relationship with Him. He also provides for those who will recognize their needs for Him, and having the courage to come and seek His counsel by making their petition clearly known to the Supreme Being, accepting the truth that when some make their earnest request known to Him, He will make known to them whatsoever they ask of Him.

In addition, having our prayer answered is guaranteed to produce a real thrill of joy and excitement just like Daniel had. His heart was filled with gratitude and appreciation knowing that God answered his prayer, and delivered him and his friends from being executed. Now in the searching of the scriptures or requesting an answer from God, it would be wise if we do not wait until our problems and trials get out of control before we take them to the Lord to solve them. We cannot afford any longer to allow our desire for personal gain to continue distracting us from becoming mature in our spiritual growth and development. Furthermore, it would certainly be a great injustice on my behalf if I do not warn you in advance about the danger of desiring to see quick victory and changes take place in our lives. Often times people's feelings automatically forces them to anticipate that they are going to have quick victory and triumph over the difficult obstacle without them hearing from God clearly. We should be reminded, however, that our relationship with Him is a lifelong process. Some victories and triumphs, therefore, may take time before we get the fulfillment, but make no mistake about this, God is faithful to His promises and His words are reliable, so be patient and allow His wisdom to establish root within your heart. It will create an inner confidence of joy and peace as you continue to devote yourselves to prayer, knowing that you have a Helper who is willing to guide you to victory over your enemies and circumstances.

Primarily, when someone is doing an investigation or seeking divine guidance they should be very careful that their searching is not motivated just for self-interest or selfish gain, but most importantly for God's interest to be magnified. Recognizing the truth that He does weigh the motives of men's hearts. Therefore, in our investigation process of seeking to get our requests answered, we must make sure that it is for the advancement of God's kingdom, and be mindful of this spiritual truth that God's love and mercy is not limited to an individual or a small elite group, but it is available to everyone. Certainly, the power of God' kingdom and authority must be understood that it is equally accessible to all who will come and converse with Him regardless of their race, background or position knowing that this opportunity was made possible by the shed Blood of Jesus. At Calvary He has purchased our redemption and granted us this awesome privilege whereby we can now approach God's throne of grace and mercy and obtain bountiful favor.

Now let's embrace this portion of scripture from Luke 11:9-13 NIV that says,

"So I say to you: Ask and it will be given to you; seek and you will find; knock and the door will be opened to you. For everyone who asks receives; the one who seeks finds; and to the one who knocks, the door will be opened. Which of you fathers, if your son asks for a fish will give him a snake instead? Or if he asks for an egg will give him a scorpion? IF you then, though you are evil, know how to give good gifts to your children, how much more will your Father in Heaven give the Holy Spirit to those who ask Him!"

Now, can you picture the power and the benefits you can get out of these three words: Ask, seek and knock? Well, they are for your advantage, if you would put them into practice. We should not gloss over them anymore as simple as they may appear or sound, but rather putting their meaning to action and see the outcome they will produce in our lives. It is only when we exercise ourselves persistently in the principles of God's word that we will be able to see effective growth spiritually, mentally and physically. Now the question is, are you longing to see God's purpose and desire fulfilled in your life? And are you daily using the revealed principles which is found in the written word of God? It is relevant to have personal inquiry of the Lord to confirm your dependency on Jesus for divine revelation. You have to totally place your trust and reliance in His knowledge and wisdom to meet all of your necessary needs for the Kingdom of God as well as your personal needs. Focus your attention on God's instruction practicing His principles and believe that He is able to offer you help.

Indeed, God provides insightful solutions and strategies through His words so that you can gain advantage over your circumstances. These problem-solving strategies are known as supernatural power and ability to apprehend the fact of the inner nature of things, whereby you are equipped to conquer and overcome the obstacles and barricades of life, that oftentimes hinder you from focusing on the things of the Lord because an individual breakthrough only takes place when you stay focused and become conscious of new discovery–important revelation that the Holy Spirit is revealing to you. Frankly, these important new discovery of revelation that you are learning is what's guiding and encouraging you to go on and become spiritually mature by taking your attention off the problems and help you to concentrate on the Lord Jesus Christ. Recognize, therefore, the truth that your effectiveness in life is totally contingent upon God's support by you listening and obeying His instruction. Know that even in the worst possible situations that one could ever imagine one must believe that God is able to bring about change when one turns to Him wholeheartedly in prayer asking for forgiveness and help.

Bear in mind that an undisciplined person do much harm to themselves, but the person who seek the Lord will find life and obtain favor. Let's focus our attention on this passage of scripture from Proverbs 8:32-36 NIV that says,

"Now then, my children, listen to me; blessed are those who keep my ways. Listen to my instruction and be wise, do not disregard it. Blessed are those who listen to me, watching daily at my doors, waiting at my

The Power Of The Carpenter's Tool

doorway. For those who find me find life and receives favor from the Lord. But whoever fails to find me harms himself; all who hate me love death."

Clearly, seeing the benefits of committing one's life to seek the Lord wholeheartedly in spirit and truth is one of the most important decision an individual could ever make here on Earth, and to make the Holy Spirit of God become the central person in their lives. The above scripture clearly confirmed the blessing we obtain when we find the Lord. It stated that whoever finds him, finds life and receives favor from Him. Just to cherish the thoughts of finding life in the Spirit should automatically produce an inspiration and motivation in your soul, an assurance that would now intensify your efforts of seeing the Lord. Officially accepting the truth that your searching will not be in vain, but rather will reveal a rewarding outcome. We acknowledge, therefore the value of our quest to validate our daily contact with the Lord by keeping our commitment and relationship active and strong. Now this is done through our regular studying of the Bible and also finding ways to apply the principles consistently in our situation, believing that God's promises are guaranteed to us as long as we keep our agreement with Him by doing whatever He requires of us. Those requests are found through the daily searching of the scripture and understanding the fact that the searching of the scripture is the key to our happiness and success. Every uninformed decision that we make create bad consequence and long-term setback especially if they are not corrected. In addition to all this, in today's world there are lots of unwise and ungodly counseling that are permeating the atmosphere seductive teaching and influences that will attract your interest, causing you to sway slowly away from sound doctrine and the path of life. For this reason you should ask God to give you the gifts of wisdom and discernment so that you may not follow any ungodly counsel that will take you into the position of downward spiral. One should know by now that all uncorrected errors are repeated in life, and some of these errors even when small destroy great opportunities. Have you ever been in the position, when a tiny error that you have been repeating in your life destroyed a great opportunity for you? It is beneficial for you to heed this advice that it can be costly if your errors once made are not corrected. Advices when given for the right purpose are very helpful and powerful, whether we get them from our peers or others. As Believers, we have a responsibility to carefully evaluate those advices to ensure that they are in line with God's standard of command. We need to invest the time to analyze the advice that we are getting by asking ourselves if it is consistent with the biblical principles of God. Let's examine what the Bereans did in Acts 17:10-15 NIV:

> *'As soon as it was night, the brothers sent Paul and Silas away to Berea. On arriving there, they went to the Jewish synagogue. Now the Berean Jews were of more noble character than those in Thessalonica, for they received the message with great eagerness and examined the scriptures every day to see if what Paul said was true. As a result, many of them believed, as did also a number of prominent Greek women and many Greek men. But when the Jews in Thessalonica learned that Paul was preaching the Word of God at Berea, some of them went there too, agitating the crowds and stirring them. The believers immediately sent Paul to the coast, but Silas and Timothy stayed at Berea. Those who escorted Paul brought him to Athens and then left with instructions for Silas and Timothy to join him as soon as possible.'*

Respectfully, in today's churches we recognize the desperate need for God's children to apply these principles and go search the scriptures for themselves just like the Bereans. This will empower them to verify and bear witness to the message of truth from the message of error which many are listening to, day in and day out. God's children need to learn how to rightly divide the word of truth from the word of error. It is a personal responsibility. Furthermore, God has made it possible for us through Jesus Christ of Nazareth, by giving us the deposit of the Holy Spirit to dwell in us, so that we may be able to discern the difference between good and evil. Therefore, we should always remember our history of how deception has always played a major role in our society, and this causes many to take offense to the gospel just like the Thessalonians. Now, there are certain people that God has strategically set up for you to come in contact with who is capable and willing to help guide you to victory but you must discern who they are, because you are called to be disciple. They are there to nurture and coach you to achieve your God's given purpose and the goal which you are seeking to accomplish. For example, Elisha asked for a double portion of his mentor Elijah's spirit and God granted it unto him because his motives were pure. We see this in 2 Kings 2:9-14 NIV that says,

> *'When they had crossed, Elijah said to Elisha, "Tell me what can I do for you before I am taken from you?" "Let me inherit a double portion of your spirit," Elisha replied. "You have asked a difficult thing," Elijah said, "yet if you see me when I am taken from you, it will be yours – otherwise, it will not." As they were walking along and talking together, suddenly, a chariot of fire and horses of fire appeared and separated the two of them and Elijah went up to heaven in a whirlwind. Elisha saw this and cried out, "My father! My father! The chariots and horse men of Israel!" And Elisha saw him no more. Then he took hold of his garment and tore it in two. Elisha then picked up Elijah's cloak that had fallen from him and went back and stood on the bank of the Jordan. He took the cloak that had fallen from Elijah and struck the water with it. "Where now is the Lord God of Elijah?" he asked. When he struck the water, it divided to the right and to the left, and he crossed over.'*

Personally, I strongly suggest that you go and read the entire chapter to get a full understanding. I urge you now, do not be deceived by worldly pride anymore. The best antidote for one to use to overcome the bad feeling of past guilt, regret, failure, and disappointment is to sincerely repent and turn to God and ask Him to give you a heart of wisdom. Success is not measured by society's standards which is fortune, fame and popularity, but rather by your obedience and faithfulness to follow godly instructions. Therefore, one should bear in mind that it is to one's advantage to appreciate the mentors that God placed in your life. They are there to impart valuable advice and share their experience with you. Respect their authority, because their responsibility is to look out for your best interest. Furthermore, when you are seeking advice make sure that you are getting it from those who are more experienced and wiser than you in the knowledge and principles of God. Also, make sure that you trust what the scripture says, above what someone claims to be true. Yes indeed, you can take advice from those who consistently practice obeying God's words faithfully.

Let's view the example of the story of the widow's oil in 2 Kings 4:1-7 NIV which says,

> *'The wife of a man from the company of the prophets cried out to Elisha, "Your servant my husband is dead, and you know that he revered the Lord. But now his creditor is coming to take my two boys as his slaves." Elisha replied to her, "How can I help you? Tell me, what do you have in your house?" "Your servant has nothing at all," she said, "except a little oil." Elisha said, "Go around and ask all your neighbors for empty jars. Don't ask for just a few. Then go inside and shut the door behind you and your sons. Pour oil into all the jars, and as each is filled, put it to one side." She left him and afterward shut the door behind her and her sons. They brought the jars to her and she kept pouring. When all the jars were full, she said to her son, "Bring me another one." But he replied, "There is not a jar left." Then the oil stopped flowing. She went and told the man of God and he said. "Go, sell the oil and pay your debts. You and yours sons can life on what is left."'*

According to this portion of the scripture, we recognize the power of the trusted advice that came from a man of God, who was filled with the spirit of wisdom. He expressed genuine concern for a hurting widow who was poverty-stricken, and on the verge of losing her two sons. Her situation was desperate, but her willingness to seek and obey sound advice from a man of God created miracles of financial freedom for her and her two sons. Today you may find yourself in a similar position, having financial difficulties, and you just can't seem to find the solution out of your debts. Well, this is your perfect opportunity for you to do what is most important and adapt the widow's principle, by seeking godly advice knowing that effective living begins with the right attitude toward God. Remember, that God can NEVER be bankrupt, so if you are seeking for help, turn to Him. He has proven His power in creation and in history. Let us, therefore, learn from the history recorded in God's Book, and build on the success and avoid repeating the failures.